D1562624

Their Mission: To Save Lives in a Sea of Blood
Combat Medic—Vietnam

HM3 Dennis Chaney, USN, Echo Company, 2nd Battalion, 9th Marines: "Medically I had done everything I could for the casualties, so I began fighting back. Using the radioman's M-16, I fired bursts at the muzzle flashes of our assailants. . . . Saving lives would take more than bandages. To save *my* people, I had to kill *their* people. It was a trade-off. . . . Finally a respite came that allowed me to get the five wounded Marines away from danger and down the hill."

Sp5c. Robert E. Bosma, C Battery, 1st Battalion, 77th Artillery, 1st Cavalry Division: "I had a job to do that no one else could do. I had to triage the casualties, sending those that I thought had a chance of living to a small clearing on the north side of the village. . . . I forced myself to ignore those I knew had no chance and whose agonizing screams hastened their inescapable deaths. Minutes turned into hours as I fought to keep those frail souls alive."

Medal of Honor Winner Sgt. Gary Beikirch, Team A-245, B Company, 5th Special Forces, Camp Dak Seang, II Corps, 1969–1970: "They came to my side, grabbed my arms, and again we went back into the inferno. Maybe it was a subconscious guilt concerning the dead baby I had treated for malaria. . . . But something drove me on (even though wounded). I had to help. I had to do what I could to save lives. All about me the Montagnards were fighting for their lives—and ours. I owed it to them."

Books by Craig Roberts and Charles W. Sasser

One Shot—One Kill
The Walking Dead: A Marine's Story of Vietnam

Books by Craig Roberts

Combat Medic—Vietnam

Published by POCKET BOOKS

COMBAT
MEDIC·
VIETNAM

CRAIG ROBERTS

POCKET BOOKS

New York   London   Toronto   Sydney   Tokyo   Singapore

An *Original* Publication of POCKET BOOKS

POCKET BOOKS, a division of Simon & Schuster Inc.
1230 Avenue of the Americas, New York, NY 10020

Cover illustration by Dave Henderson

Printed in the U.S.A.

History records the stories of the grunts—the warriors who carried rifles, machine guns, and grenade launchers—and sings praises for the combat leaders who took their men into harm's way. But it is to the unsung heroes of the battlefield, the faithful "Docs" who shared the foxholes, the heat, the trials by fire, and the terror, that this book is dedicated. It is to them—the army medics and navy corpsmen—that so many owe their lives.

Acknowledgments

This book began at midnight, October 15, 1965, in an overgrown sugar cane field bordering the village of An Trach, in the Quang Nam province of South Vietnam. After a Marine squad conducting a night patrol crossed a jungle stream to enter the village, the patrol came under intensive automatic weapons fire from a preplanned Vietcong ambush. As the Marines returned fire and assaulted into the ambushers, one Marine was wounded. The platoon's corpsman, Hospital Corpsman Third Class Lindstrom, came to the wounded Marine's aid, patched him up, and stayed with him until the enemy was routed. It has taken twenty-five years to repay that debt. Here's to you, Doc.

The author also wishes to thank those who made this work possible. Their help in the monumental task of researching and writing this book made a difficult task an enjoyable experience. My thanks to:

Wayne R. Austerman, Ph.D., Command Historian, U.S. Army Health Sciences Command, Fort Sam Houston,

Texas, for invaluable assistance in the research involving the history of the Army Medical Corps.

To Senior Chief John G. Baldwin, USN, Naval School of Health Sciences, San Diego, California, who provided a wealth of information concerning Navy Hospital Corpsmen.

To Anna C. Urband, Assistant for Magazines and Books, Media Services Division, Department of the Navy, for pointing me in the right directions.

To Lieutenant Commander Sheila Graham, USN, Deputy Public Affairs Officer, Naval Military Personnel Command, and Colonel William L. Mulvey, USA, Chief of Media Relations Division, Office of the Secretary of the Army, for their gracious assistance.

To all the fine men who took time to share their experiences with me: Sp5c. James E. Callahan, Sp5c. Michael O. Stout, HM3 Dennis Chaney, HM3 Douglas L. Wean, HM3 Lyle W. Wells, Sp5c. Robert E. Bosma, Sp5c. Stephen J. Bass, HN Timothy P. Roth, HN Leonard Finnell, and Sgt. Gary Beikirch.

And finally, to "Doc" Lindstrom, wherever you are.

Author's Note

The information contained in this book came from sources ranging from official U.S. Government documents and publications to actual taped interviews with the men whose stories appear on these pages.

This book is based upon the personal recollections of the participants and includes dialogue that was reconstructed as accurately as possible. But in a few places, due to the passage of time and the participant's not remembering the exact words, minor dialogue was inserted to match the situation, the action, and the personalities involved.

Now I shant forget the night,
When I dropped behind the fight,
With a bullet where my belt-plate should have been.
I was chokin' mad with thirst,
And the man wot spied me first,
Was our good old grinnin', gruntin'
Gunga Din.

He propped up my head,
And he plugged me where I bled,
And he gave me arf a pint of water green.
It was crawlin' an' it stunk,
But of all the drinks I've drunk,
I'm gratefulest to the one from Gunga Din.

—Rudyard Kipling, *Gunga Din*

Contents

Introduction

For the corpsmen and medics of Vietnam, the war came early. On December 22, 1961, a young Tennessee medic serving as an adviser to the ARVN (Army of the Republic of Vietnam) was riding in a truck with ten Vietnamese soldiers on their way to a distant outpost. The road seemed clear and the surrounding vegetation was not thick, but the possibility of ambush was ever-present in the countryside of Vietnam. As the truck slowly ground its way toward its destination, Sp4c. James T. Davis scanned the roadside looking for signs of the Vietcong. This was an unsecured area and they could be anywhere. In his hand, he cradled an M-1 carbine. Unlike the noncombatant medics and corpsmen who served in the previous wars of America, Davis and his fellow medics traveled armed and ready to defend themselves. He knew from experience that this war was different. It was a guerrilla war fought by terrorists who had no convictions concerning noncombatants and would not hesitate to kill a medic. In Vietnam, the words *combat medic* meant just that.

Without warning, a tremendous explosion erupted from

the roadside, sending the truck and its occupants crashing into the opposite bank. Davis was thrown clear and landed in a ditch. Still clutching his carbine, Davis scrambled for cover and took up a firing position. But the Vietcong ambushers had his range and opened up with a well-concealed machine gun. Davis returned fire until his magazine ran dry. He loaded another and within seconds, it too, was empty. He desperately ripped open another magazine pouch, but before he could extract a fresh magazine he was struck down in a burst of fire. Specialist Davis, an army medic, became the first American serviceman killed in Vietnam.

In the coming years more Americans would follow, but many more would survive because of the efforts of those dedicated medics and corpsmen who accompanied their fighting comrades into the thick of battle. Over the course of the war, 303,704 Americans were wounded as a result of enemy action. Of this number, those losing at least one limb totaled more than all those in World War II and Korea combined. Part of the reason for this is because Vietnam was a guerrilla war fought without rules. Sharpened bamboo "punji" stakes and barbed steel spikes smeared with human excrement filled holes that ranged in size from "foot traps" to those large enough to swallow two or more men. Booby-trapped trails, village huts, tunnels and jungles waited for the unwary with trip wire-actuated crossbows, grenades, cans filled with nails, broken glass and explosives, and other hideous devices. To those who were there, it seemed as if the entire country were booby-trapped. Anything that you touched might either explode or impale you. And most devices were designed to wound in a hideous fashion—not kill. In no other war in American history have soldiers been faced with such a constant proliferation of deadly devices, and almost one-third of those wounded, either by mines and booby traps or in combat, came home with a permanent physical disability.

It could have been worse. Because of the efficient and timely treatment afforded by the field medics and corpsmen, the speedy evacuation—usually by helicopter—and the advanced medical services provided in the rear area hospitals, 82 percent of those wounded in action survived. In comparison to wars of the past, this number was remarkable. But the system owed its success to the medic in the field. It was there, when the air was being torn by angry bullets and the ground shattered by artillery, that medical aid counted most. And it was there that the courage and dedication of the "Docs" was continually exhibited.

What kind of man goes to war, armed only for self-defense, with the intent to *save* lives? Is he the stereotyped conscientious objector who refuses to take up arms to kill his fellow human beings? Or is he someone who is simply doing his duty in the job he was selected to do? There is no simple answer or common ground. Each had his own reason or set of circumstances that placed him on the field of battle as a combat medic. But one thread ties them all together: the desire to help others.

On these pages are the stories told by the men who were there. Army medics and navy corpsmen who served with their comrades-in-arms from the mud of the Mekong Delta to the dust of the DMZ, and from the steaming jungles of the Iron Triangle to the rugged mountains of the Central Highlands. But no matter where they were, or when they served, they had a common purpose: to save lives. And a common enemy . . .

1

Sp5c. James E. Callahan
U.S. Army Medic
Vietnam

D*eath.* The very thought of that single word was a continuous nightmare that was inescapable. It meant the end. Finality. It could come at any time and in any manner or form. It could come slowly, stalking you like a predator hiding in the shadows, patiently waiting for a chance to strike—or quickly, in a blinding flash of light or the split-second impact of a bullet screaming into flesh. For those who had never seen it, it held both terror and a kind of morbid fascination—and hopefully it wouldn't happen to them. For the old hands who had witnessed it far too often, it became a fact of life. Something you had to live with day and night—and it could happen to anyone.

Some felt that when their number was up, there was nothing you could do about it—so why worry? Others felt that death could be cheated, or at least avoided. Just follow the rules: never volunteer, watch where you step, always use

1

cover and concealment, say your prayers, carry a good luck charm. . . .

And when those things failed, there was always good ol' Doc. *He* could cheat death *for* you. In his magic bag were the potions and tricks that would provide a barrier against the Grim Reaper. No matter how bad the situation was, no matter how intense the battle or how badly wounded you were, trusty Doc would be there. He would come through the hail of bullets, open his bag, and save your life.

But it didn't always work like that. Sometimes we failed. And when we did, men died. No matter how many times it happened, you never got used to it. When it happens you think, *Maybe I could have done something else. Maybe I did something wrong.* . . . Self-incrimination stabs into your brain in rapid-fire bursts of questions searching for answers. Then you feel rage. You blame yourself for failing and you blame the man for dying on you. Then you blame the circumstances that put you there, and finally you blame the war. The guilt has to be shared. It has to be broken up and scattered around so that no one part is too heavy a burden to bear.

For the troops, the enemy was a physical entity—the Vietcong and the NVA (North Vietnamese Army). For the medics, the enemy was something beyond a human threat that could be eliminated with the squeeze of a trigger. *Our* enemy was death itself. A medic quickly learned that it was a personal war, a war of one-on-one, Doc against Death. And sometimes the enemy won.

2

Sp5c. James E. Callahan
Alpha Company, 2/28th
Infantry (Black Lions)
1st Infantry Division
Lai Khe, 1966–1967

The Intel reports came in and the brass passed the word. Slowly at first, then gaining momentum as it stopped at each downward rung of the ladder where details were expunged because those below, of lowly status, did not have the "need to know." By the time it got to us, it consisted of: "War Zone D is 'hot.' Maybe a battalion, maybe a regiment. We're not sure. But we're going back to the bush and see if we can find them. The word is that it *ain't* going to be a walk in the park."

Operation Billings called for my battalion, along with the 1st Battalion of the 16th Infantry, to set up a patrol base with an LZ (Landing Zone) deep in Charlie country, then

3

work sweeps in the surrounding areas until we made contact. It was the normal procedure—and Charlie knew it.

For several days little happened. It was like chasing ghosts. Intel had been wrong before and maybe the area was not as hot as they had reported. We were becoming frustrated. If the Vietcong were around, they sure weren't leaving any clues. Then again the word came: We would move to a new area in search of better hunting.

The plan was simple. A clearing had been located deep in the jungle that was big enough to serve as an LZ for our helicopters, and at the same time leave enough room for the two battalions to dig in. But first the area would have to be secured. Two companies from each battalion would hump in on foot, check it out and set up security. Once this was accomplished, the remaining companies would follow by chopper. When the brass drew straws for chopper rides, we lost.

As luck would have it, Alpha Company was the lead company for the march in. I shouldered my rucksack and aid bag, pulled my helmet low, checked my .45, and fell in as the company moved out. As I took my place in the line of sweat-stained troops I silently hoped everything would stay as calm as it had over the last few days.

The farther we moved, the more I thought that the brass was wrong. It *was* turning out to be a walk in the park. I began to relax more with each step and prayed that our luck would hold. For three hours we moved, struggling under the weight of our rucks and cursing the heat. To escape from the heat and the drudgery of the march, my mind wandered back to the series of circumstances that placed me on this trail in a country that only a few years before, few at home had ever even heard of.

I had never planned on being a medic. In fact, when I joined the army, I enlisted for Europe expecting to serve in the infantry or tanks or whatever came up. But they gave us all the infamous aptitude test and my score was, as the test results stated, geared to medical service. So after basic training, instead of Europe, the army sent me to Fort Sam Houston, Texas, for medical training.

The Advanced Individual Training School for army medics lasted eight weeks. During that time I found myself sitting in classrooms listening to lectures on topics ranging from basic first aid to triage—the system used to identify and categorize casualties in terms of their severity. The slide presentations and movies of the various bloody events that a medic could encounter were enough to turn your stomach. If one of the more gruesome movies was shown before noon chow, it had a definite negative effect on our appetites.

These lectures were interspersed with hands-on training in the application of battle dressings, splints, intravenous injections and lifesaving procedures. Though we held hopes that we would serve in a hospital or troop clinic, the overpowering thought of serving in the field with the infantry was omnipresent. The techniques and skills we were learning were geared to *field* medicine—the kind that is used on the battlefield, not a hospital ward. We knew from the amount of this training that many of us *would* receive orders to combat units. And that meant Vietnam.

Finally graduation day arrived. A dead silence permeated the air as orders were read assigning us to our next duty station. But fate intervened in my behalf and I was offered a forty-two week course at Beaumont Army Hospital to become a clinical specialist. You had to be in the top 10 percent of your class to get this school and I jumped at the chance.

It wasn't what I expected. Almost all of our time was spent in classrooms and I was becoming restless and bored. Within thirteen weeks I became disillusioned with the program and elected to drop out. My timing was bad. The war in Southeast Asia was heating up and LBJ was sending more units to Vietnam every month. Some of the units already there were beginning to receive replacements for combat losses that had been steadily mounting since their arrival. Among those losses were combat medics.

In August of 1966, I became a replacement.

My orders originally read Medical Records, Saigon, but upon arrival at Tan Son Nhut air base, I was hustled aboard a bus and shuttled to a "Repo-Depot" of smelly green tents that only handled replacements for *field* units. The area was

5

dirty, the roads muddy and the heat intense. I could see that this was a far cry from the sterile cleanliness of the hospital wards I had expected and began to doubt the wisdom of dropping out of school. There would be no office job for Callahan.

Elements of the 1st Infantry Division—the Big Red One—had been in a massive firefight just before I had arrived, and had lost many of its medics. As I had expected, my orders were changed within a couple of days and I found myself aboard a Huey beating its way to the headquarters base camp of the 3rd Brigade to join the 2nd Battalion, 28th Infantry at Lai Khe, thirty miles north of Saigon. By the end of the week I finally came to rest as a platoon medic for A Company. I reported in and was directed to meet Specialist Five Hutchinson, the company's senior medic. His greeting was not what I anticipated.

"Callahan, there's one thing you gotta know and always remember. If you don't measure up, we'll ship your butt out. Alpha Company has the best medics in the battalion and we want to keep it that way. Screw up and you're gone."

That was my "welcome" to Vietnam.

After I stowed my gear I began to explore the base camp. It was typical of many of the base camps throughout Vietnam. Lai Khe was a fortified village with the infantry companies of the brigades surrounding it, forming a perimeter. In the 28th's sector, Alpha Company was tied into the battalion on the left flank, with Bravo and Charlie companies carrying on to the right to lock in with the next battalion. Within the camp was a large airstrip with twin-engine Caribou transports and helicopters constantly arriving and departing. Beyond the bunkers, mine fields and barbed wire of the perimeter stretched cleared fields of fire, ending at a thick emerald green jungle tree line. Beyond that, I was told, were the Vietcong.

The division's responsibility was to chase Charlie in War Zones C and D, roughly an area ninety miles across and sixty miles deep located fifty miles north of Saigon. From this sanctuary of thick jungle, the Vietcong threatened not only the American and South Vietnamese bases but Saigon itself. General Westmoreland had determined that the area could not be pacified and occupied by U.S. forces on a permanent basis. It could only be penetrated by large ground and air forces conducting temporary operations. "Search and Destroy" became the word of the day. Go in, try to find the VC, and kill him. Then get the hell out. And today was another of those operations. We were searching. But would we find anyone home?

The pace of the march had been fast and even with our heavy burdens, we made good time and arrived at the objective sooner than we anticipated. So far, nothing had happened and we had been lucky. So had I. Since my arrival in Vietnam a few months before, I had treated a few minor wounds, held sick call and given shots for the various diseases found in Vietnam. But I hadn't had anyone die on me yet. I dreaded the thought of that happening. I knew that sooner or later it could—probably would—happen. But I dreaded it. I just wanted to put in my time and go home without facing the prospect of someone dying because I didn't do the right thing or couldn't do enough to save them. A grunt had to eventually face his first "trial by fire." A medic had something else to face: his "trial by death." Deep inside, I knew that men died in war and often there was nothing you could do about it, no matter what you did or tried. The other medics had told me this. They tried to lessen my anxiety. It didn't help. Each day I prayed I would not have to look into a dying soldier's face. So far, God had listened. Today would be different.

As we entered the clearing, a wide kidney-shaped field of knee-high saw grass, I could see that the barren expanse was surrounded by dense jungle thick with trees and underbrush. A weird feeling came over me. If the VC were around, *this* would be an ideal place for an ambush. The only fields of fire were those from the jungle into the clearing. *Not* the other way around.

One by one, weary soldiers appeared out of the jungle, spreading out as they entered the field. Officers and NCOs began reorganizing their platoons and directing them toward designated points around the perimeter to establish

7

defensive positions. We had just entered the most critical phase of the movement. If something was going to happen, now would be the time. The remainder of our force was just lifting off in helicopters back at the first base camp, and if shit hit the fan before they arrived, we could find ourselves in a world of hurt. And within minutes, we did.

Almost everyone was out of the jungle when the first shot cracked across the clearing, turning only a few heads when it did. Then another shot, and another. Sporadic sniper fire. Not unusual. A few orders shouted by sergeants sent a couple of fire teams skirmishing toward the trees to deal with them. We turned our attention back to setting up as each company trudged through the knife grass to occupy its assigned sector.

But it wasn't just sniper fire. We had caught a Vietcong regiment in the midst of preparing an elaborate ambush for us, and the entire clearing was the kill zone. Our arriving early had panicked the Vietcong who now scrambled to assemble their troops and bring all their weapons to bear.

It soon became obvious that more than a few snipers occupied the surrounding tree line when automatic weapons, first on the right flank, then on the left, joined the incessant *pop . . . pop* of the rifles. Stunned soldiers dove for the ground seeking cover as heavy machine guns opened up from the trees and hosed the landscape. But there was no cover and no place to go. We were trapped. We couldn't move forward and we couldn't move back. Riflemen caught in the open fell in each burst of enemy fire. I knew what was coming next. And it did. Screams of pain were followed by urgent cries of *"Medic!"* Across the field I could see lone figures jump to their feet and sprint toward the calls for help, aid bags grasped tightly in their hands. So far, none of the people around me had been hit and for a few minutes I could continue to be a spectator.

In confusion and disarray, the units caught in the open scrambled to find cover from which to defend themselves. First one, then another began shooting back at the ominous jungle. The return fire pinned us to the earth and cut the grass over our heads. We had to make do with what little differences in the ground we could find. Any shell crater, any hole, no matter how small, was quickly occupied.

I crawled through the grass in search of refuge and quickly found a fellow medic, Mike Stout, almost filling a small mortar crater nearby. There wasn't much room but it was the nearest hole I could find. I squeezed in.

From every direction the volume of fire increased. We had never run into an enemy force this strong. It had to be the VC regiment Intel said existed. We had finally found them. Or they had found us.

If they broke through our thin defenses it would only take a moment before they would be swarming over those of us caught in the middle of the field. I pulled my .45 and jacked the slide, chambering a round.

"What are you gonna do with that?" asked Mike. "Take on the whole gook army?"

I looked down at my little pistol just as a burst from a 12.7 millimeter machine gun ripped overhead. He was right. I holstered the gun and peeked over the edge of the hole to see if the troops along the ragged perimeter were still holding out. They were.

"You keep sticking your fucking head up, you'll get it blown off!" cautioned Stout. Then, after more calls for medic sounded in the distance, "We've got to get out of here and find a place to get to work."

Behind us, a finger of trees that appeared to be in lower ground jutted into the field. Maybe there we could find a spot that would offer protection from the grazing fire. We crawled out of the hole and inched our way toward them.

Just before reaching the trees we came across a slight depression. It wasn't much, but it was all we had. This would have to be our aid station. We quickly set up, opened our medical bags and prepared to receive the wounded.

We didn't have to wait long. They came singly at first, dragged in by buddies out of breath from the effort, then in groups of two and three. Mike and I treated each according to his wounds and moved on to the next. As we did, bullets buzzed so close to the ground that we were forced to slither on our bellies like snakes between the casualties to keep from being hit. The machine gun and AK-47 fire continued to rip across the clearing, interspersed by the roaring hiss of RPG-7 rocket grenades that streaked by overhead and detonated in the trees behind us. M-16s, M-79 grenade

9

launchers and M-60 machine guns of the Black Lions replied in kind as the soldiers fought desperately to hold out.

Then I heard helicopters. The cavalry had arrived. I was elated at the prospect of reinforcements and "dust-off" for our wounded. I looked up to see the huge green CH-47 Chinooks circling lazily overhead. But as they started their descent they began drawing fire. In the noisy machines the pilots had no way of knowing how bad it was in the LZ. Only that it was "hot." A few tried to land but were quickly waved off by embattled GIs. They were big, slow targets that would quickly succumb to the intensive fire. The 12.7 and RPG could easily turn them into flaming coffins, killing an entire platoon with one hit. As they banked away all hope of reinforcements and dust-off faded. I felt sick.

But fear had finally run its course. With the departure of the helicopters, a sense of rage set in among those who had been too long pressed into the earth of the kill zone. It was like getting punched in the nose a few times. After the initial shock and pain, you lose all fear and begin punching back for all you're worth. The battalion commander sized up the situation and quickly came to the conclusion that we had had enough of this shit. Grabbing the radio, he called for a "danger close" artillery barrage and air support.

Within minutes artillery rounds began screaming in, impacting in the tree lines in a monstrous rolling barrage that uprooted trees in thunderous eruptions of earth and smoke. Others fell, cut in half by shrapnel, as the deafening concussions of the exploding projectiles slammed across the field. The acrid smell of burnt gunpowder lingered in the air and drifted across the field. It smelled good. I thought about the cannoneers who fired the rounds. With the number of batteries being fired, they had to know that we were in heavy contact. They would be shoving 105 rounds into the hot breeches of the guns as fast as the tube recoiled and the breechblock opened. And they were *our* guys, firing rounds made in *America.* Maybe we couldn't get our helicopters in, but the gooks damned sure couldn't stop our artillery. Someone nearby screamed defiantly at the distant trees: *"How do you like that shit, Charlie?"*

When the barrage lifted, the howl of jets could be heard as F-4s streaked in to drop their bombs and napalm on the guerrillas. Other planes joined in on strafing runs, lacing the trees with long strings of cannon and machine-gun fire. After each pass, the fire from the jungle momentarily ceased as the VC took time to recover. I wondered how anyone could survive such a pounding. But they did. Following each lull, the incoming fire quickly resumed its former intensity.

Mike and I were far too busy to worry about the way the battle was shaping up. The wounded were streaming in faster than we could handle them. Some had been so close to the impact zone that they were singed by the napalm, while others had been struck by shrapnel from the bombs.

One man was brought in who appeared to only have a minor wound in his side.

"How do you feel?" I asked as I checked his wound, a small shrapnel hole with very little bleeding.

"Okay, Doc. I can make it." He winced.

"Good. Here," I said, handing him his rifle, "guard us while we work on the others." I knew that diverting his mind and giving him something to do would keep him occupied and lessen his discomfort. And by the look of his wound, there were far more serious cases that demanded immediate attention. But appearances can be deceiving.

I left him standing guard and crawled to the next casualty. This one had shrapnel wounds from either grenades or bombs—it was hard to tell—and was bleeding profusely. As I ripped the plastic envelopes off battle dressings and started patching his wounds I saw Mike dragging still another man in.

I finished with the shrapnel victim, looked around and saw that my "guard" now lay on the ground in what appeared to be an unconscious state. Something was wrong.

I crawled over and shook him. He didn't move. I felt for a pulse. It was weak and fading quickly. The tiny shrapnel wound had done more damage than was readily apparent. He was hemorrhaging internally and had passed out from loss of blood. I would have to work fast or I would lose him. My personal enemy, Death, had crept in in an attempt to claim another victim. But I wouldn't let Death win—not without a fight.

"Mike! Bring me an IV. I've got internal bleeding here!"

Stout crawled over with the IV kit as I ripped open the

11

soldier's fatigues. He was a large man but his veins were hard to find. We frantically searched his arms, then his legs. Failing there, we even tried his groin. That didn't work so we went back to his arms and finally found a vein. Mike worked desperately, and after several tries finally succeeded in inserting the needle. This accomplished, Mike elevated the bottle and life-giving fluid began dripping into the tube.

As Stout tended the IV, I began mouth-to-mouth resuscitation. After a few inflations, I checked his pulse. I couldn't feel anything. *Don't die on me!* I took a deep breath, placed my mouth over his and blew again—and again. I kept this up for a moment and checked his pulse again. *There! A beat . . . and another!* I felt a wave of apprehensive exhilaration. Then he began to breathe. *I've* won, *you sonofabitch!*

Then, just as my initial rush of adrenaline and fear of losing him began to subside, he quit breathing. I frantically searched for a pulse. There was none. Fighting back panic, I again placed my mouth over his and forced breath after breath into his deflated lungs. But it was too late. I had failed. I couldn't believe it. I had done everything I was trained to do. This wasn't supposed to happen—not to *me!* It wasn't fair. Sadness and anger overwhelmed me. I had brought life back to him and it was quickly snatched away. I wanted to weep, to scream in frustration. But there was no time. The battle was still raging all about me and the casualties kept coming.

I covered his face and crawled to the next man. I had lost one battle with Death, but the war was far from over. In all, we had fifteen casualties lined up in the depression. Both ours and others from the 1/16th. Throughout the battle, Mike and I, and anyone we could get to help, tended the wounded. There were just too many for the two of us to handle by ourselves.

Finally it was over. Three hours after the first shots broke the jungle stillness, the VC—or what was left of them—broke contact, leaving 198 dead behind. And not all managed to escape. When the battle-weary grunts swept the tree line, they found a few dazed and wounded Vietcong hiding in the undergrowth. One prisoner told our intelligence section that they knew—before *we* did—where we would be and when we would be there. We also found out that we had been up against the Vietcong 9th Division, longtime inhabitants of the Iron Triangle and one of Saigon's major nemeses.

We knew that even though we had managed to rout them with firepower and air support during the day, they could come back under the cover of darkness to finish the job. We dug in and waited.

After a restless night watching the jungle's edge for signs of a returning enemy, the exhausted survivors of the battle began to relax with the coming of day. But for Mike Stout, the horrors of battle and the stress of standing watch all night had taken its toll. He tells what happened the next day:

When the sun finally rose to announce another day, I didn't. I settled to the bottom of the bunker and closed my eyes. I didn't want to leave. I was safe in here.

"Hey, Mike, come on. Let's get some chow."

I looked up at the entrance into the face of Callahan. "No way. I'm staying right here," I mumbled, pulling my poncho over my head.

"Bullshit. Come on. Let's eat," he coaxed.

"I've had all this shit I can take. I like it in here. Go away." I'd lost it. My mind had finally seized. Fuck it.

Every few minutes Callahan came back. Each time I told him to leave me alone and go away. I was in a bad way. But, finally Mother Nature caught up with me. I had to visit the slit trench. I hadn't taken a good crap in days. I was overdue.

I had no sooner dropped my trousers and straddled the trench than one of our troops came up.

"Doc, they need you up at Battalion."

"I'm busy," I snapped. I didn't have time for that right now.

"Top says to get your ass up to Company right away, then the captain will take you over to Battalion. Something important's up," he explained.

"I don't care. *This* is more important," I groaned, trying like hell to relieve myself.

The soldier left, but Top quickly replaced him. "Stout, hurry up and get your ass over to Company *right-fucking-now!* We gotta get you over to Battalion."

"I will, Top, soon as I get done . . ."

"You're done. Now move."

"What in the hell did I do now? What's the matter?" I asked. Going to Battalion meant trouble, especially if you had to stop at Company first to collect the company commander.

"I don't know. You must be in deep shit. Now let's go!"

After a brief stop at the company CP bunker, where I was quickly dressed in a clean set of fatigues, I followed the company commander, Captain Sawtelle, and Top Ford in a hasty walk toward the battalion command post bunker.

"What'd I do, sir?" I asked sheepishly. "What the hell's going on?"

"I don't know, Doc. Must really be bad to want you up there. Any idea what you did?" he asked with a poker face.

"No, sir, can't think of a thing," I answered, running through the events of the past two days trying to find a fuckup.

As we approached the command bunker, I could see a group of officers that had gathered outside turn their heads my way. Conversation stopped as we neared.

"Jesus, Doc. It's the division commander," cautioned Sawtelle. "It's General Hay. This must *really* be some serious shit!"

My heart was in my throat as I stopped in front of the congregation. I had visions of Leavenworth, steel bars, big rocks and sledge hammers. Oh, Christ.

"I understand you were playing doctor yesterday," said the general.

"Doctor, sir?" I asked defensively, searching for a clue as to what this was all about.

"That's right. I also heard that you were ordering a colonel and his aide around like *they* worked for *you!* Is that true?"

My mind reeled. I *had* commandeered several men to help with the battle dressings during the battle. One was a full colonel. He just pitched in and started patching up men without protest and I thought nothing of it. Now the army was going to get me for this transgression. It figures.

"Sir, I wasn't really playing doctor," I said defensively, "I was just trying to do my job."

He glared at me for a moment, then a grin pierced his face. He reached toward me and I thought the end had come. But in his hand was something shiny. A medal!

"Specialist Stout, this is one of our country's highest awards for bravery. The Silver Star," he said as he pinned it on my shirt.

The Silver Star. I couldn't believe it. I hadn't done any more than anyone else had done. At least I didn't think so. I damned sure didn't do more than Callahan, and *he* wasn't there. The feeling of doom dissipated, replaced by one of question.

"I don't want this, sir. This is bullshit. Where's Callahan? He did as much or more than I did. . . ."

The general looked about in question. I looked at Top.

"Where's Callahan? He deserves this more than me," I stated somewhat forcefully. "I don't want anything unless Callahan gets it too."

"We'll take care of him later," said the captain.

"But, sir, this is bullshit. . . ."

"Stout, be quiet. You're outranked here," cautioned Top.

I *was* outranked, and there wasn't anything I could do but accept the medal. I saluted, thanked the general, did an about-face and marched away.

"Goddamn, Stout, you don't tell the commanding general 'bullshit'! Are you crazy? Jesus Christ. I can't believe it. You actually told the division commander *bullshit*," said Top as we departed the area. Captain Sawtelle began to laugh, then Top joined him. They guffawed until they almost choked. I wanted to laugh too, but my heart wasn't in it.

In the heat of the battle, Callahan and Stout did not notice a photographer snapping his camera nearby. Associated Press photographer Henri Huet caught them working over the soldier whose life they tried so desperately to save. One of the photos accompanied an article on the battle that ended up in newspapers across the country. He described the action in the caption:

A man with an abdomen wound was among the first to die. Two medics—Spec 5/C James Callahan of Pittsfield, Mass., and Spec 4/C Mike Stout of Sapulpa, Okla.—worked over him in vain.

A few words on paper. Not much of an epitaph. Not even a name. He may have been among the first to die, but he wasn't the last. In all, casualties numbered 31 killed and 113 wounded. Of the 600 men who went into the clearing, 456 remained to carry on.

After pulling back to their base camp at Lai Khe, thoughts of the nameless soldier in the field haunted Callahan. "I wondered if I had done everything that I possibly could for him. God knows I tried. But sometimes, no matter what you do, you lose. You have to live with that. But it's hard. *Damned* hard."

In a caption beneath two other photographs by Henri Huet that appeared in the *Washington Post* on Sunday, June 18, 1967, the situation was described:

DEATH IN THE JUNGLE—James E. Callahan of Pittsfield, Mass., an army medic, employs mouth-to-mouth breathing at left in an effort to save the life of a soldier in a War Zone D jungle in Vietnam. At right, realizing his efforts have failed, the medic looks up while covering the GI's face . . . the soldier who subsequently died had suffered an abdomen wound and efforts to have him removed to a field hospital were unavailing because heavy enemy fire made it impossible for a rescue helicopter to reach the area.

James Callahan had finally undergone his trial by death and had persevered. For his actions on that day he was awarded the Bronze Star Medal for valor.

3

Emerald Hell

The Vietcong were not the only killers in Vietnam. The jungles, mountains and rice paddies of the country all contain hazards that are almost as deadly as the enemy. Poisonous snakes, bloodsucking insects, life-threatening diseases and dangerous animals of every description infest the land. And as deadly as the flora and fauna of the tropics is, it is something every trooper has to contend with no matter where he is. The blazing sun beats down on you relentlessly, turning rice paddies into steaming sauna baths, open fields into reflective frying pans, and jungles into soul-sapping ovens with air so thick you have to make a concerted effort to suck in each breath. The heat is so intense that you think that at any moment your blood will boil.

Simply trying to exist in the furnace of Vietnam drains you of strength, energy and motivation. Add the weight of combat gear, weapons, ammunition, rations and radios to the men trying to traverse difficult terrain and you have the recipe for trouble. Heat exhaustion is commonplace, heat stroke as deadly a killer as the Vietcong.

Heat exhaustion causes you to slow down then begin to feel faint. You might even pass out for a few moments, then regain consciousness. Your skin will be moist—maybe even dripping with sweat—and cool to the touch. At the same time, your pulse will weaken. Normal treatment consists of someone elevating your feet higher than your head, administering fluids, covering you with a poncho or blanket, and observing you until the faintness passes. It normally is not serious unless allowed to progress unchecked.

But heat stroke is a different matter. You first feel a headache, followed by hot dry skin and a strong rapid pulse. Your temperature quickly elevates until your skin is hot to the touch, then your sweat glands shut down and your skin becomes dry. Your face turns red as blood rushes to your brain and you feel like your head is going to burst. Then you pass out.

Besides cooling your body with water—if there is any—propping your head up, possibly administering an IV and waiting for medevac, there is little the field medics could do for you in the bush. And if something wasn't done quickly to reverse the symptoms, you died.

"Doc" Mike Stout, Callahan's partner during the battle in the clearing, would find his trial by death long before that deadly day. And with it, he would learn many lessons.

"I was just a green country boy from Kellyville, Oklahoma. I didn't have much experience in what went on in the world when I graduated from high school. I only knew that you were supposed to go to college if you wanted to get ahead. I enrolled at Oklahoma State University, but my folks didn't have much money for tuition so I had to drop out and work every other semester so I could go back. The army caught up with me during one of these work periods and I was inducted on March 9, 1966.

"I went to basic training at Fort Bliss, Texas. When my company completed basic, we held a company formation to receive orders. One of the drill sergeants announced, 'The following people will go to Fort Sam Houston for medical training,' and my name was on the list.

"I thought, *No infantry training for me! I'm going to the medical corps! I'll have it* easy *compared to those guys going to Fort Polk for infantry training.* I saw myself working in some nice clean air-conditioned hospital. It never entered my mind I would be a field medic—with the infantry.

"After Fort Sam, I had a thirty-day leave. When I returned, I had orders for Vietnam. Still, I felt the possibility of serving in the field was remote. It wasn't. Within three days of arrival in Vietnam I had orders for the 1st Infantry Division at Lai Khe. Now I was scared. I had heard too many stories while I was waiting for orders and all had the same theme: People *died* out there. And it would be up to me, if at all possible, to see that it didn't happen. I wondered if I could handle it. Could I do my job? Could I *really* save lives? It was a lot to ask of a green nineteen-year-old kid with ten weeks of medical training."

4

Sp5c. Michael O. Stout
2nd Battalion, 2/28th
Infantry (Black Lions)
1st Infantry Division
Lai Khe, 1966–1967

As we hacked our way through the dense jungle that bordered Highway 13, I wondered what it would be like to save a life. That's what it was all about: *saving lives*. I hadn't done that yet. I had only been in-country a few weeks. But sooner or later I would find out. Thoughts of all the types of traumatic wounds that I might be faced with raced through my mind. Back at Fort Sam Houston we had seen the films, had the lectures, even worked in the hospital. But it wasn't the same and I knew it. Would my first casualty have a gunshot wound? Shrapnel from a grenade or mine? Maybe a puncture from a punji spike? Within moments I was to find that it was none of the above. Without realizing it, the enemy that would give me my first experience of fighting death was an enemy that had been with us all day, lurking, watching, waiting.

"Medic! Pass the word—get Doc up here!"

My thoughts of sucking chest wounds, lacerated abdomens and gunshot wounds disappeared as the word came back down the column, passed from man-to-man like an overdue bill in search of a debtor. *That's odd,* I thought, *I hadn't heard any gunshot, no explosion . . .*

I adjusted the two bandoleers of M-60 ammo that crossed my body in a fashion reminiscent of Pancho Villa—we all carried extra ammo for the guns—verified the presence of my two aid bags and sprang forward along the narrow column of troops. Something had happened, but what? *Maybe a snake bite or twisted ankle,* I reasoned as I fought my way forward through the tangle of underbrush.

The going had been rough for the company. For hours we had carved our way through twisted vines of double-canopy jungle that held the stagnant heat like a pressure cooker. Thick groves of bamboo resisted every swing of the machete, frustrating the men with blisters on their hands and aching muscles in their backs. Fighting for each step, we had progressed only by hacking a man-size tunnel-path through the emerald hell. As we struggled forward, our heads spun in weakness as the sauna bath of Vietnam sapped our strength. All about us were creatures with venomous fangs or stingers. And then there were deadly devices of the VC. At any moment a man could fall victim to shit-smeared punji stakes and spike-filled foot traps. As I struggled forward to answer the call every conceivable evil entered my mind.

"Doc, up here!" called a young soldier, pointing to a man lying on the ground. "Point's down." I brushed past him, dropped to my knees beside the casualty and began examining him.

"What happened?" I asked, looking for obvious signs of injury.

"He just passed out. Must be the heat."

He was a large black man, a strong healthy type who appeared capable of bulldozing his way through the bush without the aid of the machete he had wielded. But the all-powerful blazing sun had taken its toll. He lay there, a limp rag doll, with sightless eyes rolled back in their sockets. I felt his skin. It was hot and dry. I would have to work quickly to save him. "Heat stroke," I announced, reaching for my canteen. "Get me more water!"

He had to be cooled down quickly. If I didn't work fast, he would die. I emptied my canteen, pouring it over his body to allow cooling evaporation, then emptied the next canteen passed to me. I paused to watch for a positive reaction. There was none. Then he began to choke and hack. Something was interfering with his breathing. *Vomit! Oh my God!*

I worked his jaw open and started clearing his mouth, scooping out vomit with my fingers. But before I could finish, his breathing stopped. *Don't panic! Get air into his lungs!*

I was never what one would call prejudiced. Growing up in the Oklahoma hills, I had never been around blacks. Until I was drafted I had only known one black person, the sole Negro in my high school. All the other students were either white or Indian. But after some unpleasant encounters in the army, I just stayed away from them altogether. Now I had one whose life depended on me and I was the only one who could save him.

My training took over. Without hesitation, I began mouth-to-mouth resuscitation. It was my job—my responsibility. The sickening smell of vomit, the slick foam of saliva and the stink of the rotting jungle assailed me as I squeezed his nostrils shut, took a deep breath and clamped my mouth over his. Again and again I forced air into his lungs, watching his chest rise and fall with each inflation. Finally, after what seemed like an hour but was in reality only a few minutes, he responded. Slowly at first, then beginning to stabilize more with each breath, he began breathing on his own. I checked his pulse. It was faint but was returning. I sat back with a sigh of relief.

"Get on the horn and get us a dust-off. We gotta get this man out of here," I ordered as I unrolled a poncho to use as a stretcher, "and get me some bodies up here to help carry him to the LZ."

Waiting for the chopper, my mind recounted the events. I was a cherry to combat—an FNG (Fucking New Guy)—

and he was my first casualty. No battle dressings, no morphine, no trauma—not exactly what I had expected as a *combat* medic. Yet I had saved a life. The men of Charlie Company had watched me while I worked, wondering if I would measure up, if I could hack it. I had—so far. I did what I was trained to do and it had worked. I felt good. But I knew that heat was only *one* weapon in Death's arsenal.

As days turned into weeks, I found that a medic's job called for more than just following the man in front of him on sweeps and patrols and worrying about heat casualties. One of our missions concerned area security and was as deadly as any firefight. Clearing the mines from "Thunder Road," as Route 13 came to be known, was a daily task. The road, little more than a dusty ribbon stretching north from Lai Khe, was mined almost every night by the VC, then cleared every morning by the 1st Infantry Division. After each clearing operation, convoys of ARVN trucks raced up and down the road transporting troops and supplies to their various camps. But before the trucks would roll, we had to do our job. Each morning found the battalion trudging out to sweep the road, then doubling back on patrols in the jungle on each flank of the "highway" for ambushers. Once cleared, we would set up linear security along the road until the trucks passed. This operation continuously put us in harm's way and Charlie took every opportunity to rain on our parade.

It was still morning when we completed our company sweep of the designated area, established our security and began sending out platoon-size patrols. I settled in with the company headquarters element—the captain and his RTO (Radio-Telephone Operator)—to fend off the heat and boredom as much as possible. Minutes dragged into an hour. Finally, the patrols called and advised that they were at their farthest checkpoints and were starting back. I took a swig of warm chemical-tasting water from my canteen, swatted at pesky mosquitos and waited. I would feel much better when they were all safely back. I glanced at my watch, estimated the time it would take for the patrols to return and tried to make myself as comfortable as possible. As I settled my aching back against my grounded rucksack the radio crackled with a transmission from one of our platoons in the bush.

"Charlie Six, this is One-Six, over?"

The RTO picked up the handset and pressed the transmit button. "This is Six-Kilo. Go."

"This is One-Six. We're about five hundred meters out and we've found something out here. We're gonna check it out." I recognized the voice of Staff Sgt. Ed Greene, the platoon sergeant. A friendly and helpful NCO, Ed had given me both assistance and advice whenever I needed it. He was good in the bush and an excellent combat leader. When he was out, there was usually little to worry about. His men respected and trusted him. I had accompanied him on many patrols and we had developed a close friendship. I listened to the radio exchange intently.

"One-Six is on their way back in, sir. They've found something and are going to check it out," relayed the RTO to Captain Paone, Charlie Company's commander.

"All right. Tell 'em to set up security and watch their ass," advised the captain.

"Yes sir," acknowledged the RTO, keying the mike. "Six says 'Be careful.' Charlie Six-Kilo, out."

Within a minute I heard the explosion. A tremendous *crump* in the distance shattering the jungle stillness jerked me to full awareness.

"That was in the direction of One-Six, sir," exclaimed the radioman. The radio came to life and proved him correct.

"Six, this is One-Six. We need help! We need a medic! Jesus, we need help now!"

I sprang to my feet. A young buck sergeant grabbed his weapon and joined me. "I'll go with you, Doc. Charlie might be waiting for you."

"Take off, Doc. I'll saddle-up the company and be right behind you," Captain Paone called after me as I sprinted toward the road.

I darted toward the east where One-Six was supposed to be, the sergeant taking point. We crossed the road and entered the jungle, making good time until we came to a rice paddy full of slimy water that stretched almost a hundred yards to the next tree line. I studied the distant row of vegetation. A wispy black haze hung in the air over the trees.

"That must be where One-Six is," said my partner.

"It'll take too long to go around," I said, misjudging the depth of the paddy. "Let's head straight across."

"Okay, Doc. I just hope there ain't no fuckin' snipers around."

We plunged in and began slogging through the paddy, our feet calf-deep in sucking muck, warm water rising to our waists. I tried to run, but running was impossible. Crossing rice paddies is a fight, not a movement. Each step was a struggle. It was exhausting, and soon I felt myself growing weak and dizzy in the heat. Only adrenaline kept me going.

As we drew near the opposite bank, I could see people on the ground. Finally, after struggling through the man-made swamp for what seemed like a mile, we came to the edge. Fighting my way free of the clinging mud, I crawled up the embankment to One-Six.

"It's bad, Doc. We found a claymore and it was booby-trapped," reported one of One-Six's troopers, pointing to the scene of carnage. "Ya gotta do something!"

I ran to the first victim, a young redheaded kid named Garland Fugate, and immediately knew there was not much I could do for him. He was purple, evidently caused by the concussion from the backblast of the claymore mine. Even though it appeared obvious that he was dead, I checked for a pulse. There was none.

"He's dead," I announced, more to myself than to those about me. Fugate only had a week left in his tour. He was due to rotate home and had been harassing everyone in the company that morning about "being short" with only a week to go. He was right. He was going home—early. I moved to the next man, a Spec Four named Strandberg. It was immediately apparent he was now a soldier in the gray land of death. "He's dead too."

"Over here, Doc!" A short distance away, a trooper pointed down at a fallen comrade. After the first two casualties, I expected the worst as I scurried to his side.

"Jesus," I whispered, looking down into the pain-stricken face of Ed Greene. "Jesus Christ!"

"Give me morphine, Doc. Give me morphine. I can't take it. It hurts," he pleaded.

"Okay, Ed. Hang on," I answered, tearing my aid bag open. "You'll be all right, buddy. I'll get you taken care of." I wasn't sure that I could. He was bad. He had taken the initial blast of shrapnel, but he was conscious. Maybe, if I did everything I could, I could save him.

I tore his shirt open. Several pieces of shrapnel had penetrated his chest and abdomen. From the groin area down, he was hamburger, totally shredded. I had never seen anything like it. I began to have my doubts, but maybe, just maybe . . .

I gave him morphine, stopped what bleeding I could, and called for medevac. *Maybe if I get you back to the hospital in time,* I thought, my mind screaming obscenities against fate.

As I worked on Ed the remainder of the company caught up with us. Riding on armored personnel carriers with the 1st of the 4th Cavalry, also on road security, they had skirted the rice paddy and now rumbled out of the bush to a halt.

"Medevac's on the way, Doc. I'll have 'em land on that dike," yelled Captain Paone, pointing to a wide dike in the paddy.

"Okay, sir. We gotta get these people out of here in a hurry. We've got two KIAs already."

I did what I could for Ed and moved to the next casualty. I was almost in a state of shock over Greene's condition, but had to carry on. There were still more wounded to be handled.

Pfc. Spina, a young kid from Philadelphia, had adopted me when I came to Charlie Company. Always trying to show me something or give me a lesson in bushcraft, he continuously tried to help out "old Doc."

"Just pay attention, Doc, and I'll teach you things you'll never forget," he would say. And this day he would.

Spina lay on the ground, blood soaking his left breast. I ripped his shirt open, quickly exposing a small shrapnel hole bubbling pink with blood. A sucking chest wound. I tore open a battle dressing, jerked the plastic cover off, and placed it on his chest. I covered it with the battle dressing and taped it down. This one I could save.

Looking him over, I determined that there was no other damage. "Spina, you'll be just fine. We're going to get you out of here to the hospital, but they'll just do a little patch job and you'll be back in no time."

"Okay, Doc. Thanks," he replied with a weak grin.

I treated the last casualty, Pfc. Howe, by digging shrapnel out of his ass. He was the least injured of the wounded and I knew there would be no problem with him. I went back to Greene to do what I could to keep him stable until the dust-off came. Within a few minutes I heard the beating of the Huey's rotor blades.

That evening we returned to the base camp. Captain Paone walked up, his face sullen. I knew something was wrong.

"Doc, Howe made it okay."

"I knew he would, sir. How are the rest?" I asked, fearing the worst.

"They're all dead."

"Dead? That can't be, sir. Spina should be all right—he just had one minor chest wound and I handled that. . . ."

"He's dead, Doc."

"No!"

I had to know what happened, what went wrong. He shouldn't have died. Someone had to have made a mistake. I finally found out. Someone *did* make a mistake. Me. Spina had not one, but *two* wounds: the one I treated, and a second I never saw. In his armpit, impossible to see without raising his arm, was a second tiny hole that penetrated his lung, causing his lung to collapse. I had rolled him over, checked him back and front, and found nothing else. But I didn't raise his arms. If I had found that wound he would still be alive. My mind reeled. *Goddamn! From now on I'm going to strip every wounded man if the situation permits, and check every* inch! Spina had definitely taught me something I would never forget.

Mike Stout rotated home from Vietnam on August 23, 1967. His next duty assignment was on an ambulance team at the Chemical and Biological Warfare Center at Fort McClellan, Alabama.

5

Medevac

Vietnam had the most efficient medical evacuation system of any war in history. With the proliferation of helicopters within the country and the speed of the jet transports for the long-distance runs, the battle casualty of Vietnam stood a better chance of survival than those of any previous war. A man wounded in battle could be on an operating table in a field hospital or larger medical installation within minutes. From there, he could be evacuated to Clark Air Force Base in the Philippines in less than two hours, Japan in less than six and the United States in under twenty.

The tiered evacuation system first introduced at the Battle of Antietam in the Civil War had come a long way. In Vietnam, a soldier could feel confident that the platoon corpsman or medic would reach him almost immediately if he was hit. Then, after being stabilized, and action permitting, he could find himself being loaded aboard a medevac helicopter that, if not already standing by nearby, would normally arrive within twenty minutes of being called. And as soon as the helicopter lifted off and banked away, he would enter the most advanced medical triage and evacuation system known to any military organization in the world.

Depending on the type and severity of the wound(s), the casualty would either be taken to a field hospital or a rear area hospital. If the field hospital was selected, it was normally a cluster of green canvas tents stretched over wooden frames with plywood floors. Here, teams of surgeons were ready to sort the casualties in order of severity. Those with the most life-threatening wounds were handled first.

The triage process continued beyond the treatment stage. Those cases requiring additional care that was more time-consuming or beyond what the field hospital could provide were sent on to either rear hospitals or hospital ships cruising off the coast. Those that could be treated and returned to duty from the field hospital were kept there until they were released to return to their units.

Cases requiring treatment at a rear area hospital, a permanent installation of either buildings or Quonset huts, would go through another stage of triage: Those that could be treated there and returned to duty would be sorted from those that would be treated and sent on to large hospitals out of the combat zone—usually Japan or the Philippines.

The casualties leaving the combat zone fell into two main categories: Those who would recover and be immediately returned to Vietnam, and those who would require a longer period to recover or were too disabled to return to combat duty or remain in the military. The latter would go home.

For the men who found themselves on Military Airlift Command C-141 Starlifters on their way home to "The World," it was often a depressing journey. Though they were glad to be leaving Vietnam, many were returning home crippled, blinded, disabled or missing one or more limbs. And some were simply going home to die. One medevac casualty describes the long flight from Japan to Travis Air Force Base near San Francisco:

"It was weird. Those of us who were ambulatory sat in

29

seats in the front half of the airplane while the guys on stretchers were stacked on racks in the back half. Since our seats faced the rear—I guess for safety in case we crashed—we spent the entire flight facing the guys on the stretchers. Most were pretty messed up. There were a few that were missing an arm or leg, and one guy had his whole head bandaged up. Others had bandages wrapped around their chests and stomachs. IV bottles hung everywhere and tubes were stuck in several of the guys.

"I could tell that some of them were in real pain and were moaning. But I couldn't hear them because the plane was so noisy. After a while, two air force flight nurses that looked old enough to be my grandmother came by and gave us box lunches. Inside was a cold piece of chicken, an apple, a can of fruit juice and some potato chips. It was the best meal most of us had eaten in a year. Beat the hell out of C rations. But as I ate my drumstick, I looked up at the guys on the stretchers. They didn't get any food—probably because of abdominal wounds and such—and I felt sorry for them.

"We had been issued new khaki uniforms that didn't even have any stripes or anything. We looked like a bunch of new privates, except our hair was longer and we were tanned and thinner. The uniform shirts had short sleeves and none of us had any underwear on—we never wore it in Vietnam—and the plane started getting cold. It just got colder and colder and pretty soon we were freezing. And it stayed that way all the way to Travis.

"When we landed it was night. The trip took about seventeen hours, and because there were no windows in the plane, it seemed that we had been in the dark the whole way. When I limped off the plane the first thing that struck me was all the lights. There were lighted buildings and streetlights everywhere. After a year of pitch-black nights in Vietnam it was really weird—but it was beautiful, the most beautiful thing I had ever seen. And there weren't any parachute flares in the sky and no rumble of distant artillery—only car horns and the sound of traffic. It was just too much.

"As I stood on the ramp taking all this in, a bus and some ambulances drove up and guys started getting in to go to the hospital. Several medics walked up the back ramp of the plane and began carrying stretchers off. I watched them as they walked by and saw that one casualty had his face covered with a blanket. I asked what happened and was told that he had died just before we landed. I felt sorry for him, not just because he died, but because he never saw the lights."

The journey didn't end at Travis. Casualties were now divided into two groups. The first were those that would recover over a period of time and return to duty plus those that required watching to see if they *could* return to duty—and if not, be medically discharged. The second group were those that would *never* return to duty and couldn't be cared for at home until a certain amount of therapy had taken place.

The first group went to military hospitals on active military bases that either specialized in a specific area of treatment, or to the military hospital nearest the patient's home of record if no specialized care was required.

The second group was not quite as fortunate. Consisting of amputees, cripples, paraplegics, quadraplegics, men who had been blinded, and everyone else who could never reenter active duty, they found the Veterans Administration hospital nearest their hometowns serving as the final stop. Most VA hospitals were understaffed and inadequately equipped institutions that simply served as the storage houses of the damned. And though the majority of the veterans sent to the VA hospitals were eventually released to go home if there was a hope that they could make it through life on their own, the remainder would spend their lives in these institutions—human reminders of the war in Southeast Asia.

No matter how far through the system the casualties went, they all started in the same place: on the battlefield. And the first link in the chain of events that involved their care was the man who came to their aid in complete disregard for his own safety. For before the casualty would even hear the beat of rotor blades of the approaching dust-off, a combat medic or corpsman would have already performed the necessary tasks to keep him alive long enough to reach the first stop on the long road home. In the majority of cases, without the medic in the field, the remainder of the system was worthless.

6

Sailors in Green

Unlike the army, which has its own medics, the Marines are supported by medical corpsmen trained and supplied by the navy. Each Fleet Marine Force infantry company has a senior corpsman and one or more platoon corpsmen in each platoon attached. These sailors in green, often after joining the navy to serve in a hospital or aboard a ship—and many to avoid the war in Vietnam—found themselves wading the rice paddies, climbing the mountains and hacking through the jungles alongside the grunts in some of the most dangerous places in Vietnam.

Navy medical corps training for the young sailors began at the Hospital Corps Schools at either San Diego, California or Great Lakes, Illinois. These schools were much more intensive than their army counterpart. Because navy corpsmen often found themselves posted in remote stations or aboard ships or submarines far from outside support, they were trained to handle almost any medical problem that might arise. In World War II, there are eleven reported instances of enlisted hospital corpsmen performing appendectomies aboard submarines far at sea—all of which were successful. On surface vessels of the fleet that are too small to justify a ship's doctor, the hospital corpsman *is* the doctor and must be able to handle any type of injury or illness until the ship nears a port or larger vessel to which the patient can be evacuated.

Hospital Corps School, known as Class A or simply "A School" in navy terminology, is the basic medical training school for enlisted personnel. In four months the students undergo training in such subjects as pharmacology, patient treatment, physiology, anatomy and all forms of patient care as it relates to working on a hospital ward. During this time each student receives plenty of hands-on training by working on actual wards. Battlefield medicine comes later. At the end of A School, the class is divided—often alphabetically—into groups going to advanced, or B schools. These might be surgery tech, operating tech, pharmacy, X-ray tech, or other specialized fields. A certain percentage, depending on the demand, go to the Marines. And during the years between 1965 and 1971, this usually meant Vietnam.

But before the corpsmen selected for duty with the Marines arrived in Vietnam, they had to complete one final school after their months of medical training. To prepare the young corpsmen, Field Medical Service School, run by the Marines in the rugged hills of Camp Pendleton, California, or Camp Lejeune, North Carolina, awaited.

Hospitalman Third Class Dennis Chaney elaborates:

"As a sailor, you just didn't volunteer for the Marines, show up one day, and get issued a set of greens by some smiling supply sergeant. There was no 'welcome aboard, Doc. Glad to have you,' until you paid your dues. And the dues were high.

"The fraternity on the campus of USMC with the motto of *Semper Fidelis* made its pledges undergo a selection process second to none. And for us, the transplaced sailors with the medical bags who had arrived from San Diego, the process began at Camp Pendleton.

"Formerly a Spanish ranch of the old California days, Camp Pendleton jutted out of the Pacific coastline of southern California in a series of steep treeless razorback ridges dotted with scrub oak trees, cacti and dry brown grass. Nothing was level. It was either uphill, or downhill. And that's the way the Marines liked it. We hated it.

" 'This is a far cry from what I expected when I joined the navy,' I said to one of my classmates as my eyes roamed across the ragged landscape.

" 'Yeah. This ain't exactly a big comfortable ship.'

"A big comfortable ship. That's what we had envisioned when we enlisted. And what better job to have on that ship, or at least in a shore duty assignment, than that of medical corpsman. A ship or a hospital. That's the way to spend a war. But this?

"As we contemplated our fate, a fate dictated by the fingers of faceless clerks who sit in secure offices, typing up pieces of paper stamped "Original Orders," a big burly Marine sergeant strutted up to our waiting formation, came to a halt and set his shoulders and jaw. A hush fell over the formation as he began to speak.

" 'Working with the Marine Corps is not something that comes easy. It takes a special breed to do the things the Marines are called on to do. We don't receive any easy missions. They're all tough. As corpsmen attached to the Marines, you have to be as tough as the men you are supporting. Here, at Fleet Marine Force Field Medical School, we will do our best to teach you what you need to know to accomplish your mission, and hopefully enough to keep you alive in combat. We can't make you into Marines in four weeks, but we'll get you as close as we can. While you are here you will participate in forced marches, bivouacs, weapons training on rifles and pistols, and other combat-oriented classes geared to keep your ass alive and functioning on the field of battle.

" 'I have a detachment of Marines that will act as both casualties and patients, and when needed will be the aggressors when enemy forces are required. Learn from them. Ask questions. Practice your skills here. You'll need this education later, I can guarantee you.

" 'If it gets too tough, if you think you just can't make it and want to drop out, forget it. The only way out is to be washed out for physical or mental limitations. *We* will make that determination, not you. If *we* determine you can't cut it with the Marines, you're gone.'

" 'I don't think I'm gonna like this place,' I whispered out of the corner of my mouth.

" 'No shit,' replied my friend.

"But most of us made it. After a grueling four weeks humping mountains and slogging down beaches under the weight of full packs, shooting the weapons that we hoped we would never have to shoot for real, facing multiple 'casualties' wearing mulages—artificial wounds made from rubber to resemble the real thing—conducting triage, and navigating cross-country with nothing but a map and compass, we found ourselves physically and mentally tougher than we ever thought possible. We had the ability to go that one extra step. None of us knew at the time just how important that ability would become in the months ahead. For the entire class—unknown to us at the time—was destined for Vietnam."

Dennis Chaney was destined for more than Vietnam. His duty assignment took him to the far northern province of I Corps, just south of the demilitarized zone. Attached to the 9th Marine Regiment, the famous "Walking Dead," Chaney would find himself with the Marines in places with strange names that would burn their places into American military history along with Guadalcanal, Iwo Jima and Tarawa. Names like: Con Thien, the Rockpile, Leatherneck Square, Cam Lo and Camp Carroll.

Here, the Americans faced more than the crafty bands of Vietcong that refused to stand and fight unless cornered. Only a few kilometers away was North Vietnam—and the NVA who infiltrated the border on every opportunity.

On December 17, 1967, HM3 Dennis Chaney walked into a war that was reaching its greatest intensity since the Marines landed two years before. It was almost too much for a young corpsman to take.

7

HM3 Dennis Chaney
USN., Echo Company
2nd Battalion, 9th Marines
Quang Tri, 1967–1968

I was terrified when I arrived at Camp Carroll, the Marine combat base near the village of Cam Lo. The words of the rawboned, tanned Marine at the airport at Phu Bai had given me more than just a bit of apprehension. He had overheard me talking to Gene DeWeese, my buddy who had gone through Corps School with me, as we waited to board the C-130 that would take us to Dong Ha on our way north to join the 9th Marines at Carroll. It was obvious that he had been in Vietnam long enough to know what he was talking about.

"Two-Nine? That's the 'blood bucket battalion.' "

"Blood bucket battalion?"

"Yeah. They've lost more men than anyone else. They're a real meat grinder. They're in the worst part of the whole damned country—up north, right near the DMZ."

And from what I could see, it appeared he was right. This definitely was a combat zone. Surrounding the main area of hard-backed tents were artillery pits, concertina wire laced with claymore mines, wooden watchtowers, bunkers and red dirt. The amount of sandbags that had been filled and stacked was tremendous. Everything was fortified. The Marines didn't build a place like this unless they expected bad things to happen. And where bad things happen, a man needs an abundance of luck—or maybe a guardian angel. Mine appeared when I reported to Echo Company.

"Anything you need, Doc, just ask," said Lieutenant Carson, my new platoon commander. "We take care of our Docs. Just do your job and take care of my men. Above all, Doc, don't sweat the program. I'll take care of you. You'll be just fine."

I felt much better after Carson's friendly welcome. He seemed like a capable fellow and one that was sympathetic to the needs of his men. For the first time I began to relax a bit. He didn't seem worried and appeared to have the situation under control. Maybe everything would be okay after all.

"Where do you want me when we're on patrol or whatever?" I asked.

"Just stick to me and my radioman. That way I can send you where you're needed."

Stick with Carson. No problem. I could handle that. After all, he was going to take care of me—and I would take care of his men. Very simple. Very basic. Just do my job and everything would work out. After all, I would have a whole *platoon* of Marines around me. What could happen?

Within a week I found myself, encumbered by a heavy flak jacket and steel helmet, following Carson's sweaty green-clad men on a company sweep in the area between Camp Carroll and Cam Lo along Route 9. Things went well until about nine o'clock in the morning. As we began to approach a knoll marked on the map as Hill 37, I heard a strange sound break the stillness of the morning. A whistling *whoop-whoop* of something flying through the air, quickly followed by a cracking *crump* as it hit the ground, jerked my attention away from the thoughts of discomfort caused by my heavy burden. The first explosion was followed by another, then another as a barrage fired by unseen gunners began bracketing us. Each eruption of red earth was quickly replaced by black smoke and falling debris. Marines broke from the file and began darting for cover screaming, *Incoming . . . incoming!*

Mortars. Tubes that launched projectiles in an arc that kept the enemy gunners safely out of sight. The Marines called them "high-angle hell." They had our range and now began firing in earnest. Explosions rocked the earth and crept closer with each blast, but we didn't stay around to greet them. Orders were quickly shouted and we began withdrawing to safer ground.

Across the small valley sat a pimple on Vietnam's butt known as Hill 38. From there, we would be out of range of the infernal weapons and still close enough to have an advantageous view of 37. And it was "high" ground. At least one meter higher than 37.

The company pulled back across the valley, climbed the hill and finally we reached the top. From our meager perch we scanned across the defile to Hill 37 where the mortar fire had originated. We could see movement, but couldn't tell who they were. A Combined Action Platoon was supposed to be stationed there and something had obviously gone wrong. As I knelt near the radioman, the company commander made several futile attempts to contact the CAP unit by radio, but to no avail. There was nothing left to do but try and reach them on foot. Hopefully the mortars had pulled out in fear of counterbattery fire. They seldom stuck around after the initial barrage. Without knowing what the status of the CAP unit was, we would have to go back to investigate.

After crossing the valley, we followed a path up the hill to the gate of the first defensive string of concertina wire. My ears were attuned for the sound of incoming that never came. I began to relax. Ahead of me, the radioman jammed his handset to his ear and again tried to rouse the CAP unit. But after several attempts failed, the captain grabbed the handset and began issuing orders to his platoon commanders.

"Two-Six, this is Six actual. Take your people around to the right and get on line. As soon as we can determine what we're up against we're going up."

A short acknowledgment in crackling squelch from Two-Six, then the captain squeezed the rubber transmit button again. Two-Seven would go left.

Marines cautiously moved off to the north and south, their weapons at the ready. But just as we began to deploy, the crack of rifles and the buzz of bullets announced the enemy's presence. The little men with AK-47s held the high ground above us and it would be rough going if we tried to advance. But still, the captain had made up his mind. The Marine Corps is assault oriented and that's exactly what we were going to do. But before we could organize the assault, fire broke out from the bottom of the hill *behind* us. We were caught in a deadly crossfire, a dilemma that had not happened by accident.

Beyond the valley, a convoy from the 11th Engineers had been moving toward Camp Carroll on Route 9, the road that snaked its way between us and the NVA element to our rear. The NVA had seen them coming and waited. When the trap closed they, like us, were caught in the middle. In what seemed like minutes the entire convoy was wiped out. Bullet-riddled trucks lay scattered about the road in smoking hulks. And with them were the wounded and the dead.

Trapped, we could not react to assist them. We had our own problems. The NVA now closed another side of the deadly box, sending a high volume of fire our way from the right flank. Then the dreaded call came: *Corpsman up!*

With my Unit One aid bag dangling from my shoulder, I sprang to a crouch and began sprinting across the east side of the hill toward the calls for help. But I didn't get far. Halfway across a clearing, I was spotted. NVA gunners shifted their fire, pinning me to the ground. I tried to move, but each time I did a fresh burst of fire kicked up spurts of dirt in front of me and hammered the earth to my flanks. I tried to raise my head to locate the source of the fire, but each time bullets ripped just over my helmet, pressing me into the ground. I was terrified. I couldn't move toward the casualty, and I couldn't pull back. Caught.

Then, as I thought the end was near, the NVA gunners shifted to other, more lucrative targets that had appeared. I grasped the opportunity and began moving again. I inched my way to the wounded man and began bandaging his wounds. It was the radioman. He had been hit twice and was bleeding profusely. As I worked, the battle intensified. But finally, with the help of other Marines, we managed to carry him farther down the hill to relative safety. Then, before I could start back up the hill, another sound penetrated through the staccato bursts of gunfire. Engines.

Overhead, "Puff, The Magic Dragon," a converted C-47 transport armed with Vulcan cannons and other magic stuff, circled the field of battle. Quickly analyzing the situation, the crew ejected canisters that hit the ground spewing smoke to confuse and blind the enemy.

As the smoke spread, the noise of the airplane was joined by the sound of approaching choppers. Huey gunships banked in and began spraying the hill. But because of the smoke obscuring the terrain, they couldn't tell friend from foe. They began spraying everything that moved. But, as miracles so often happen, no Marines were hit.

As I hunkered behind a large boulder with the radioman and four other wounded Marines, incoming fire fixed our position. Medically, I had done everything I could for the casualties, so I began fighting back. Using the radioman's M-16, I fired bursts at the muzzle flashes of our assailants. Fear was rapidly being replaced by anger and an ingrained instinct for survival. Saving lives would take more than bandages. To save *my* people, I had to kill *their* people. It was a trade-off.

The NVA were close. I could hear them talking and shouting orders just on the other side of the boulder. I returned fire as well as the situation allowed. I emptied one magazine and quickly reloaded another. I had to protect my wounded men—and I had to survive. Finally a respite came that allowed me to get the five wounded Marines away from danger and down the hill.

After reaching the bottom of the hill where the wounded were being staged, I began taking stock of the injured. It was time to be a corpsman again. I began applying more battle dressings and administering morphine sulfate from little tubes, pinning the empty tubes to the collars of the wounded with the needle so the hospital people in the rear would know that they had already received a dose of the potent drug.

Other wounded Marines were scattered all over Hill 37. When I finished doing what I could for the men at the bottom of the hill, I went back up to the scene of the firefight and made my way from casualty to casualty, doing what I could to patch up each man. Finally, toward evening, an enterprising Marine drove up in a six-by truck that he had found abandoned on Route 9 and we began loading the wounded. But the battle was not over. The NVA still controlled the crest of the hill.

Our company commander was gung ho—too gung ho. He was not going to let a bunch of little men with AKs keep him from taking his hill. He wanted the hill, no matter what the cost. Again we started up.

Marines fought their way forward, and when we reached the concertina wire, he ordered men to throw their bodies across the wire, flattening it so other Marines could run across to storm the top of the hill. But the grunts balked. They thought that it would be a useless gesture that would cost Marine blood to satisfy someone's ego. Air strikes and artillery could do what was needed.

Finally, after realizing that a major command problem existed, he backed off from the order and pulled what was left of the company back to reorganize. Later that evening, when the situation was more favorable, Echo Company took the hill.

When the last of the wounded was loaded aboard the truck, I climbed in for the ride to Cam Lo, the nearest village held by friendlies. A small CAP garrison defended the village with a small contingent of Marines and Vietnamese, and there we would be able to land helicopters for medevac extraction.

It was getting dark when we drew close to the village. But instead of the expected safe haven, we found ourselves in the middle of another battle in progress. Cam Lo village was under siege. Huts were burning and I could see flames licking into the darkening sky. The hammering of machine guns and the crackle of rifles echoed across the landscape. Tracers streaked along the ground, occasionally striking hard objects that caused them to ricochet into the air in burning trails of red and green, finally disappearing high overhead as the phosphorous burned out.

It was mass confusion. NVA had penetrated the village and were running about shooting civilians, torching huts and throwing grenades. The pungent smell of gunpowder lingered in the air mixed with smoke from burning straw from the hooches. A feeling of despair overwhelmed me as the hope of a safe haven evaporated.

The driver, quickly analyzing the situation, pressed the gas pedal to the floor and blasted through the village at full speed. We had collected more wounded before we left the hill and now had seventeen on board. Many lives were at stake and every second counted. We had to get them through.

Pop-up flares filled the night sky illuminating the way as we raced between the burning buildings. Inside the CAP compound at the center of the village Marines and their Vietnamese counterparts fought valiantly. The throaty bark of heavy fifty caliber machine guns countered the NVA fusillade and M-16 fire punctuated the bursts as each Marine did his duty.

The driver jammed on the brakes as we approached the CAP compound gate. With all the confusion in the dark, we could easily be mistaken for the enemy and killed by "friendly fire." One of our Marines dismounted, threw his weapon down and advanced toward the gate with his hands in the air. Staring into the ominous snouts of two fifty caliber machine guns, the Marine stopped.

"Hold your fire. We're Marines . . . Echo Two-Nine!" he yelled.

"Get your asses in here!" yelled one of the gunners, his face barely visible over the smoking barrel of his gun. "The gooks are everywhere."

Jamming the truck into gear, the driver let out the clutch and floored the accelerator. The truck bolted forward into the compound, the gate quickly closing behind us.

Cam Lo village was now an inferno. NVA and Vietcong ran around at will shooting and killing. Bodies lay scattered everywhere, many draped over the concertina wire of the compound, mute testimony to the fanatical human wave attacks of the NVA in their determined effort to wipe out the small unit behind the fence. The CAP Marines had taken their toll of the enemy and were still desperately fighting to repulse the determined attackers.

Inside the small compound was an area large enough to permit helicopters to land. Perhaps we could still get a medevac in. But for the moment, since I found that I was the only corpsman there, I had more urgent responsibilities to the wounded. My seventeen, and now several of the wounded CAP people, needed immediate attention. As I crawled from one to another, I came to one of my guys, Joseph Applegate, who was shot up so badly that I immediately knew that there was little I could do. He was dying. As I bent over him, I could hear the distinct sound of blood rattling in his lungs as he struggled to gasp for air. I examined his body. It was a bloody mess. How could he possibly breathe with so many wounds through his chest and the very essence of life flowing so freely from his body? As I bent over him he grabbed my flak jacket in a viselike grip. His eyes locked on mine, his face contorted with fear.

"Doc, please don't let me die!" he pleaded.

I didn't know what to say. What can you say to a dying man?

"Doc, please don't let me die . . ."

He pulled me closer, pleading with me like I could stop the inevitable. I put my arms around him and held him tightly—hoping that he could feel my presence. At least this way it might feel like there was someone close by to help him cross over to death. He wasn't alone. No one should die alone.

Finally, he took in one last breath, and as he exhaled I sensed his life leave his body with the air from his lungs. His grip relaxed and his hands fell from my jacket. His eyes stared vacantly at the black sky like windows in an empty house. I witnessed for the first time what had been described in so many stories as "the last dying gasp." An incredible feeling of helplessness came over me. Then I got mad. All he wanted to do was live—and I had let him down. It was *my* fault. It was *his* fault. It was *the enemy's* fault. It was the *whole damned war's* fault.

"I won't let you die!" I shouted into his face. I forced his jaw open with one hand, pinched his nostrils closed and began mouth-to-mouth resuscitation. I was his faithful Doc. I had to do something. Even though I knew it was hopeless, I had to do something—for me if not for him. I had to try.

Reluctantly, after exhausting myself by going through the motions of CPR to absolve my guilt, I accepted the fact that he was gone for good. But it wasn't fair. I'd done everything I had been trained to do that day and had been rewarded with this. I was numb.

But I had little time for self-pity. There were others to tend. I grabbed IVs and began searching for veins. I replaced blood-soaked bandages, checked pulses, administered medicines and did what I could to comfort my charges. Then, just after three in the morning, the battle slackened. Firing tapered off and men began emerging from their positions to take stock of the aftermath. As more casualties were found, Marines began bringing them in. All told I had twenty-seven wounded. I was exhausted. For too long adrenaline had kept me going. Now it was beginning to wear off. My mind was beginning to become muddled with fatigue. Then, as I began to question how much longer I could go, I heard the welcome sound of the first helicopter as it made its approach to the landing zone.

We loaded the most critically injured first, then triaged the next load. Another chopper appeared and they too disappeared into the night for the hospital at Dong Ha. By first light the last load was evacuated. With this group went Joseph on the first leg of his long journey home.

In the stillness of morning I walked across the smoking battleground. NVA bodies littered the compound and village, some twisted in grotesque positions. Weapons lay scattered about, now useless tools of war. A bulldozer belched diesel smoke and began scraping the red earth. Shortly, a trench was opened that was large enough to hold the dead. Marines dragged NVA bodies to the edge and roughly pitched them in. Dead meat in uniforms, they thudded to the bottom in grisly heaps.

"Hey, Dennis!"

I looked up to see who had called my name.

"Gene!" I shouted. "Where in the world did you come from?"

Gene DeWeese! I couldn't believe it. If he was here, it meant Golf Company, the unit he had been assigned to, was here. The cavalry had arrived.

"Heard you guys needed a hand, so Golf came to the rescue. You look like hell."

I looked down at my tattered uniform. I was covered with dried blood and filthy with sweat and crusty dirt.

"You should have been here last night," I tried to joke. "It *was* hell."

8

The Breaking Point

When old men send young men off to fight, it is usually to achieve a goal: defend a country, defeat an enemy, protect a border or expand a boundary, or, in the case of Vietnam, help a friend. Yet, for those who must go, what begins as a noble crusade in the beginning often loses its significance in the dirt of the battlefield. But until they have seen it for the first time, it is something foreign—and intriguing.

Vegetius, a military scribe in ancient Rome (A.D. fourth century) wrote: "No great dependence is to be placed on the eagerness of young soldiers for action, for the prospect of fighting is agreeable to those who are strangers to it."

But after the first battle, when blood is spilled and lives are lost, men—especially young men—change. It's when you see death up close, when you see it in the blank stares of the faces on the bodies of what once were your friends, that it comes home in the blinding realization that there is no such thing as immortality. If it happened to them, it could happen to you. The child loses his innocence and enthusiasm and, through the most brutal of processes, becomes a man. Howard Fast, in *April Morning*, wrote: "And you've

lost your youth and come to manhood, all in a few hours . . .
Oh, that's painful. That is indeed."

And the pain, for some, deepens with every encounter
with the face of death. One begins to question his sanity and
wonder how long he can take it. Surely there's a breaking
point, but when will that point be reached?

For each individual it's different. Some become hardened,
losing compassion for others as they build a mental shield to
protect themselves. A "better him than me," attitude begins
to prevail. And it worsens as time goes by and more horrors
are witnessed. To those in combat whose lives seem to
progress from one battle or operation to the next, feelings
are further numbed by each experience. Killing and dying
become the norm. "How many dead?" asks Siegfried Sas-
soon in *The Effect.* "As many as ever you wish. Don't count
'em; they're too many. Who'll buy my nice fresh corpses,
two to a penny?"

But the "Docs" found it hard to lose their compassion.
They *had* to care. It was their job. No matter what they
witnessed, what they had to endure, they had to persevere
and carry on. Too many people depended on *them.* Still,
they were only human. And humans have a breaking point.
For the medics and corpsmen, that breaking point hovered
nearby, a constant companion.

*And ye shall hear of wars and rumors of wars. See that
ye be not troubled, for all these things must come to pass,
but the end is not yet . . . for nation shall rise against
nation and kingdom against kingdom . . . but he that
shall endure unto the end, he shall be saved.*

—Matt. 24:6–13

9

HM3 Dennis Chaney, USN

The longer I was with Two-Nine, the more I began to question my sanity. With each horror, each death, I changed. It was like there was a circuit board in my brain with a row of buttons that controlled my sense of mental balance and values. Each time I witnessed something horrible a button was pushed that put me closer to losing it. All of it. After four months in Quang Tri Province half of them had already been pushed.

On April 6, we drew a mission to recover the body of a dead recon Marine who had been killed on Hill 190. Reinforced with another platoon, we crossed the Cam Lo River by helicopter to effect the mission. The Marines never leave their dead and would expend great efforts to recover them. No matter what it cost.

After locating a suitable LZ on the side of the hill, the helicopters landed and we dismounted for our search for the dead Marine. Cautiously, we began moving toward the spot on the map where the body was thought to be.

We didn't know it but we had been detected as soon as we'd landed. An NVA spotter relayed our coordinates to his guns, and within minutes artillery and mortar fire began falling around us. Marines scattered for cover as each shell burst in a geyser of red earth. Then as quickly as it started, it ended. Why would they do that? They had us and let us go. It didn't make sense. The sudden silence shocked us. My eyes darted across the hill in apprehension. What were the bastards up to now?

We quickly located the dead Marine and the lead element approached to make the recovery. As they bent over their fallen comrade a tremendous explosion rocked the ground. Marines simply disappeared. In their haste to retrieve the body, they'd failed to check for booby traps. The body had been rigged to a five-hundred-pound bomb.

The explosion from the bomb left a huge crater. Closest to the crater was what was left of five Marines. Outside of that circle were forty more who'd fared only slightly better. Every conceivable wound, every type of traumatic damage, covered their bodies.

"Corpsman up!"

A needless call. I was standing near the radioman, only a short distance from the scene, when the whole thing erupted before my eyes in full color and stereo sound. The concussion had slammed into me, almost knocking me to the ground. I *knew* I would be needed as soon as it happened. I shook off the initial shock and ran toward the smoking crater.

Along with the other corpsmen that accompanied the platoons I began frantically separating the casualties by the seriousness of their wounds. Helicopters circled overhead and one-by-one settled in for medevac. As I was preparing one man for evacuation, a young Marine ran up.

"Doc, you better come quick. The lieutenant's pretty bad," said the Marine, his face in shock.

I followed him to where his officer lay on the ground. He had been close to the explosion and shrapnel had changed his life forever. Both legs had been blown off just above the knees, leaving ragged stumps from which short segments of bone protruded and bright red arterial blood pumped in spurts with each beat of his heart. The first lifesaving step taught at Corps School exploded in my brain: *Stop the bleeding!*

I tore open my aid bag and pulled out two tourniquets. Working as quickly as possible, I wrapped each thigh above the wound and tightened the straps. Finally the bleeding stopped. The second lifesaving step followed: *Treat for shock!*

The lieutenant was talking coherently, which meant that the pain had not set in yet. The damage was so traumatic that it would be a moment or two before the realization and the pain would come over him. When it did, he would go into shock. Only morphine would keep that from happening. I pulled a syringe from my bag and gave him an injection.

I knew that if we didn't get him to a hospital before the morphine wore off, he would die. I quickly unrolled a pole-less stretcher, a nylon affair with handles sewn into the sides, and spread it on the ground next to him. Then with the assistance of others, I gently moved him onto it.

As we carried him down the hill, one shattered leg bone kept jabbing me in the back of my thigh. With each step, the bone struck me. A wave of sadness came over me, quickly joined by anger. I felt sorry for him, but I was angry for myself. How much of this can a man take? Will the horror and dying never end? Instead of being the saviour of the living I was becoming the clearinghouse for the dead and wounded.

"Keep taking those pictures," said the lieutenant. I looked around to see what he was talking about. The morphine had taken effect and he had entered that state of euphoric giddiness that the drug provides. He had given a camera to one of his men who walked next to us and was giving him instructions as we made our way down the hill. "Take a picture every step of the way. I want this whole thing on film. I want to remember what happened here."

I couldn't believe it. It was just too bizarre. Something in my mind clicked, like a button being pushed that dampened my feelings, but at the same time made me feel that my sanity was escaping. I was a caring individual and becoming hardened didn't fit my personality. It was a defensive mechanism that, for me, was having adverse effects. I knew that eventually I could reach the point where no buttons remained. When that happened, I would surely go insane. Hopefully my tour would end first. If it didn't, I would.

As soon as the lieutenant was loaded on the medevac chopper I started back up the hill. There were still more wounded to handle, triage and carry back to the LZ. I had learned a lot in the few months I had been in-country, and one of the things I had discovered is that the corpsman could not carry enough bandages to go around if things got really thick. I made sure each Marine carried two battle dressings on each operation. If I was out of them, then there were still more to be had wherever I was needed. That practice saved a lot of lives that day.

I reached the scene of carnage and joined two other corpsmen who were moving from one casualty to the next. Everybody was busy. Marines were carrying wounded down the hill, radios were squawking orders and questions, officers and NCOs ran about attempting to bring order to the chaos, and medevac choppers flew low overhead, arriving in relays to extract those that were ready for transport. On the perimeter of this activity Huey gunships nosed over to launch rockets, and F-4 Phantoms streaked in to lay napalm in a concerted effort to keep any enemy elements off our backs. If we were hit now, it was questionable if we could be combat-effective with the few troops that remained. And of those, even fewer could be spared to fight.

Many of the remaining casualties had "sucking chest wounds." Of all the types of trauma induced by projectiles, a hole in a lung is one of the most serious. Internal bleeding, and worse, the possibility of a collapsed lung, would kill. I ripped open plastic envelopes that kept the battle dressings clean and slapped the packages over bare skin to seal the wounds. Then on top of the plastic, I applied the dressing covered with adhesive tape to hold it in place. I kept repeating this procedure as I discovered more and more men with holes in their lungs, air whistling in and out through the jagged holes. Plastic, dressing, tape. Over and over.

After the last man was evacuated from the field of death, we corpsmen finally boarded helicopters for the welcome flight home to Camp Carroll. I looked out of the door of the Sikorsky at the hill below as we banked away. It looked very peaceful, almost beautiful, from this lofty perch. Hell didn't look so bad—from a distance. But then, neither does an ugly woman.

You could get away with a lot of things in the Marines, but some transgressions were seriously frowned upon. Among those that fell into the purview of corpsmen were the Marines whose combat effectiveness was diminished due to a microorganism. Gonorrhea, or the "clap," as we called it, took its painful toll on more than one unfortunate leatherneck. Not only did the troops find female companionship in the local village, but they occasionally smuggled Vietnamese "boom-boom" girls into the camp itself.

Two-Nine had standing orders concerning the clap. If anyone ended up with the clap more than once, they were busted in rank. Because of this, I treated quite a few cases on my own on the qt. I knew what dosage of penicillin to give and who was allergic to what. Finally, Dong Ha began wondering about the amount of penicillin we were going through without proper log entries in the BAS (Battalion Aid Station). As I had by now inherited the job of senior corpsman, I was ordered to educate the Marines on the hazards of sex with the locals. After giving classes and orientations on the horrors of VD to the Marines I began lecturing my corpsmen.

"We gotta get these guys to quit messing with these girls. Dong Ha is not going to buy any more of my excuses on the amount of penicillin we're going through. It's up to us as corpsmen to get this—if not stopped—slowed down to a trickle."

"A trickle? How about just a drip?" said one of my men with a laugh.

"You know what I mean," I snapped. "I need some help with this."

I felt like maybe we were becoming effective in our campaign against the clap until one day not long after.

"Hey, Dennis," called one of my corpsmen, entering my tent.

"Yeah? How's it goin'?"

"Got a little problem."

"Oh? What's that?"

"Got any more penicillin?"

"Some. Got someone who needs a shot?" I asked, digging through my medical supplies.

"Uh huh. Me," he answered sheepishly.

"You? *You?* What do you mean? *You* have the clap?" I asked incredulously.

"Just gimme the damned shot."

"Drop your trousers, sailor. Quit your grinnin' and drop your linen. Of all people, you shoulda known better."

I actually enjoyed giving him the jab.

After five months in Vietnam I felt like I had seen it all. With each casualty that I treated, I became more hardened. I had finally learned how to deal with the sights of traumatic injury and death. At least I had convinced myself that this was so. June 5, 1968, would prove me wrong.

Echo Company had been assigned the mission of maintaining security between Ca Lu and Khe Sanh. It was supposed to be "kickback" duty for us, but we spent quite a bit of time on patrols in the vicinity. As senior corpsman I didn't have to go. I had other corpsmen I could send. But I needed the break and it was a way to spend time with the guys in the field. I was more comfortable doing that than sitting in the rear area.

We were crossing a river on our return march back toward Cam Lo when the platoon's new radioman, a black Marine named Harry Thomas, slipped. The weight of his equipment took him under and he didn't reappear. We scanned the surface of the water frantically waiting for his head to bob up, but it didn't.

Marines fanned out along the banks in case he washed ashore while I and two other Marines quickly dropped our gear, stripped our clothes off and dove in to try and find him. I was almost in panic as I swam out into the current.

This just couldn't be happening. I *had* to find him. If we got to him soon enough I might be able to save him.

I went under again and again, feeling in the murk with my hands. Minutes dragged by. Following each dive I swam a little farther out and dove again. After several minutes of this—diving, searching, feeling—I came to a large rock. I submerged again and swam toward it. As I got close my hands touched clothing. It was Harry. He had been stopped in the current by the rock, his body suspended on the upstream side. With the help of the others, we pulled him up and dragged him to shore. I examined him quickly. No pulse. Harry was dead and mouth-to-mouth resuscitation and heart massage would be of no use.

Harry was my friend and a good Marine. It was hard for me to accept the fact that he died in such a way in the middle of war. It was one thing to die in combat, quite another to succumb in such a useless manner. It was like when your number was up, it was up. No matter where you were or what you were doing. Still, it just wasn't right. Sadness and depression gripped me, squeezing my soul with icy fingers.

I took Harry back to Cam Lo. There was now a Battalion Aid Station set up there and when I arrived, there was a lot of activity. A helicopter had been shot down on its approach to the tiny base and burned on impact. The pilot's body had been brought in and was badly charred. The horrible smell of burnt flesh permeated the air, assailing my nostrils and clinging to me like a nightmare I couldn't wake up from. Between losing Harry and seeing the pilot, I felt that one more step in losing my sense of humanity had taken place. My mind began shutting down. I felt like I was finally beginning to lose it. Sanity was escaping me and there was nothing I could do about it. Another button on the control panel of reality was being pushed. While I stood there trying to hang on to what little values I had left, the battalion surgeon walked up.

"Chaney, I've got some bad news."

"I don't need any more bad news, sir."

"A jeep was knocked out yesterday afternoon by an RPG

round. It was leading a convoy of new replacements out to the field when it was ambushed," he informed me, as gently as he could.

I had to ask the question, but was afraid to ask. Finally, "Who was in the jeep?"

"Lieutenant Carson."

"No! It can't be!" I sobbed. I felt like I had been hit in the head with a brick. *Not Lieutenant Carson!* The man who had taken extra measures to take care of me all the time I was with his platoon, my friend—my guardian angel—it couldn't be! He was *my* officer and I was *his* Doc. Marines always took care of old Doc. I had my pick of C rations, my choice of where I slept, anything I needed to do my job. He saw that I had the best of what could be offered. He even assigned his radioman to be my security, sponsor and protector. Lieutenant Carson not only took care of me, he took care of *all* his men in the same manner. The company commander who'd demanded the folly on Hill 37 had finally been relieved and Lieutenant Carson, being the senior lieutenant in the company, had taken temporary command while we waited for a new captain. As such, the convoy escort had fallen to him.

It was all I could take. I was burned-out. The war had finally become senseless to me. The idealistic young sailor who came to a country to help the oppressed became the aged corpsman who finally realized the insanity of war—a war where young men killed young men for the aspirations of old men. I no longer wanted to help the Vietnamese— which had been my justification when I first arrived—I only wanted to survive and do what I could to see that my Marines survived. When I began carrying more ammunition and grenades than battle dressings I knew it was time for me to get out of there. But the choice wasn't mine. I had to stay until the powers that be issued the orders to send me home.

Until that happened, I knew that I had knowledge to impart to new men—advice that might save their lives, but advice embittered by my experiences. When new recruits came in, I gave them what wisdom I could, then answered questions. One young man looked at my gear, his face a question mark.

"I didn't know corpsmen carried grenades, Doc. Aren't you supposed to be a noncombatant?" asked one green arrival.

"Yeah. But this war is different. I carry two. Know why?" I asked.

"No."

"One for them, and one for me. No way I'll ever become a prisoner. The NVA don't care if you're a noncombatant or not. They'll shoot anybody."

"Jesus."

As I looked at his young face my mind drifted back to Field Med School at Camp Pendleton and jungle orientation in Okinawa. The indoctrination we received didn't come close to preparing us for this place. The patriotic crusaders who landed months before had become dispirited, morose and cynical killing machines. War has a way of bending the human spirit to the breaking point—and sometimes beyond. Values learned in peace too often change in war. I had changed and so would the new guys. They just didn't know it yet. We tried to prepare them for what was to come as well as we could, but some things just couldn't be described adequately. Only personal experience in the field would fill in the gaps. And only experience would make them hard enough to survive.

With Lieutenant Carson's death, *I* found the real meaning of becoming hard.

We left Cam Lo on July 8. The remainder of the month and all of August found us at such places as Con Thien, Cua Viet and Gio Linh and combat zones in between pulling operations and sweeps. It seemed that for us Vietnam would never end until we were dead, shipped home in a rubber bag. Everything we did, everything we saw, reinforced this opinion. Then came the operation—a sweep reinforced by tanks—that took us to the DMZ. Though I had been living in hell all the time I had been in Vietnam, I found that like Dante's Inferno, hell was a series of levels, each worse than the previous. In the DMZ I saw what the bottom level looked like. A B-52 raid had come in and carpeted the landscape with bombs and what remained was almost indescribable.

"Look at that!" said one of the grunts, pausing to scan the pockmarked terrain as we came upon it. "Ain't nothin' left out here."

The entire valley had been flattened. It appeared like a huge hand had descended out of the heavens, scooped up the earth and slammed it back down upside down. Every tree had been reduced to a stump not over six inches tall. As far as the eye could see nothing remained of the lush green countryside of Vietnam. It was the epitome of death and destruction. Gigantic bomb craters turned the once beautiful terrain into a vast wasteland that reminded me of pictures of the surface of the moon.

We stood in silence and tried to comprehend the massive amount of ordnance that had to have been expended to create such a scene. Then I detected a familiar smell. The bombing had been preceded by napalm and the odor of the burnt jelly still filled the air. It clung to the lining of your nostrils and worked its way into the weave of your utilities where it would stay for days.

The silence was overpowering. No birds sang, no monkeys chattered, no pigs squealed. and no dogs barked. I felt that we had stumbled into a verse right out of Revelations. Compared to the damage we could inflict with our puny rifles and grenades, this was a preview of the Apocalypse. As I looked across this sterile world a question entered my mind that screamed for an answer: *Why didn't we just fight this war with air power?* My Marines were dying for ground that could be taken with impunity from the clouds. Another button had been pushed.

The operation continued. We came across caches of uniforms, equipment and rice. Then, as we progressed deeper into the Zone, we began finding enemy emplacements and a few dead NVA. But so far contact eluded us. It wasn't surprising; nothing could have lived through the devastation caused by the B-52s.

I began to relax as we moved on. That was a mistake. Just as we started across a fairly level area we made contact.

Ragged rifle fire opened up on our flank, followed by RPG (rocket-propelled grenades) that shrieked by, missing their mark. If it was an ambush, it was poorly planned and poorly led.

We took cover and began returning fire. As I watched the grunts maneuvering for better positions, I could tell that the enemy was not up to their usual efficiency in the way this attack was conducted. It was a puzzle and a piece was missing. Though the shots gradually drew closer to the Marines' positions, they had a long way to go to become effective.

Before they *could* become effective, one of our tanks clanked forward, spun to face the attackers, then, instead of firing the main gun as I had expected, charged the NVA. All shooting stopped as we watched in fascination and curiosity. The tank raced on, throwing dust and dirt in a billowing cloud from its tracks as it churned across the kill zone. The NVA shot at it desperately for a moment, then stopped shooting when they realized that the lumbering beast could not be stopped.

The tank crew never fired a shot. Instead, they bore down on the NVA bunker until it disappeared beneath their treads, collapsing as the fifty-two-ton machine passed over it. Then, in reaction to too many past frustrations and uncounted desires for "payback" by the crew, the tank turned, came back to the position and stopped on top of it. As I watched, the green monster began to turn in circles, slowly grinding the NVA ambushers into the ground.

I raced forward with the others to check for prisoners, not that we expected anyone to survive, and was incredulous at what I discovered. There, in the bottom of the nest, I found the answer to why the ambush seemed conducted by amateurs. It was because they were.

They were kids. Twelve- and thirteen-year-old kids. Intelligence would say that the NVA were getting desperate, that they were running out of troops. Maybe so, but a kid with an AK-47 or an RPG could kill you as dead as a veteran soldier. I *knew* that. But *why* did they have to use *kids*. *Damn* them. As I stared at the carnage, I felt another button being depressed.

We took one prisoner. An interrogation followed.

"He says that there was an ambush set up three klicks away, sir. They were expecting us, but we ran into this element first."

A few more questions from the interpreter followed, then the answers.

"He also says that many NVA are coming down, even as far south as Con Thien, dressed as women—riding water buffalo."

The NVA weren't running out of troops. And the war would never end.

The promised replacements for us corpsmen didn't come as expected at the end of six months of field service. The promise of six months in the field and six months in the rear at a medical battalion, which was the plan when I arrived in Vietnam, never materialized. But at the end of the ninth month, the navy finally realized we still existed and welcome replacements began to arrive. My reprieve had come.

"Get on the chopper, Doc. You're being transferred out of the field!" yelled Staff Sergeant Petty, our platoon sergeant. "You made it!"

I was incredulous. I grabbed my gear, waved at the others and sprinted toward the waiting machine whose rotors were already turning in anticipation of flight. I stopped short of the door and looked back. The familiar faces of the Marines I had treated, and who guarded me like a virgin sister, stared back. And as I looked, I saw the hint of a few smiles—and maybe a telltale wink. Their way of saying, "Good-bye, Doc. And good luck."

Little did I know how much I would miss being with these guys in the coming weeks. In the field, there was no petty harassment. At Third Shore Party's BAS at Quang Tri, it was unlimited.

"You pukes get this placed squared away. It looks like a shit house," screamed the chief. The chief, a short stocky olive-skinned Italian, was a stickler for doing everything "by the book." His penchant for harassing the troops earned him the moniker of "Little Caesar." He strutted and yelled constantly, making life miserable. Though we had been pulled back to Quang Tri for the long overdue stand-down, it wasn't long before those of us that had been in the field, and had grown to hate it, began to actually miss it. At least in the field you didn't have some petty dictator wake up every morning with the sole intent of tormenting the troops. And in this case, there was more than one tyrant to contend with.

Third Shore Party Battalion at Quang Tri was a far cry from the medical battalion we had expected. Stationed in the safety of the rear, the Shore Party Marines were an arrogant bunch who acted like they were in garrison in the States. Most of them had not been in combat and had no idea what was happening in the field, yet they strutted around like bantam roosters looking for a fight and talked a mean game. Little Caesar was no exception.

Yet, as bad as he was to work for, the Shore Party gunnery sergeant was worse. He hated corpsmen. We were navy and he was Marine. In his mind, natural enemies. Every day proved that compared to him, Ivan the Terrible was a model child. Life in Quang Tri was more unbearable than in the field. At least there, you could *kill* the enemy.

But in the military, what goes around comes around, and there's always a time for payback. And for the tyrannical gunny, payback came when he finally drew R and R (rest and relaxation).

"Gunny's on his way over to clear BAS for R and R," said one of our guys, smiling. "He'll be out of our hair for a week!"

"Wait," another corpsmen said, "this is our chance to get even."

"What do you have in mind?" I asked.

"It's shot time."

It didn't take long to burn his shot record. Without it, he would have to take every shot in the book to clear base for leave. And we knew it.

"Gunny, uh . . . there's a small problem here," I mumbled, flipping through his medical file.

"Yeah? What?" he demanded in a growl.

"Well, seems your immunization record has been misplaced. It's not here," I informed him, closing the file.

"Whatta ya mean, it's not there?"

"It's not, Gunny. Don't know what could have happened. Looks like you'll have to have all your shots over again." I bit my tongue to keep from cracking up.

"All my shots . . ."

"Yeah, Gunny. Before you clear base, you have to be caught up. But, there's good news too. We've developed a serum that will give you all your immunizations in one shot."

"One shot?" he asked, looking more hopeful.

"Just one," I said, turning to pick up the syringe. I turned around, and his eyes grew wide. In my hand was a fifty cc syringe and cardiac needle—a hypodermic as big as a tire pump.

"Drop your trousers, Gunny, and we'll get this over with."

Without hesitation, and with a tirade of obscenities, Ivan the Terrible spun on his heel and marched directly out of the BAS.

"I ain't gonna take *that* just to go on R and R. You squids can just get screwed!"

For the first time since our pullback to Quang Tri, it wasn't the "squids" that got screwed. The Gunny never *did* go on R and R. Funny what a "little" syringe full of sterile saline can cure.

Incidents like this helped lighten our load. At least no more buttons were being pushed. Still, the three months at Quang Tri lasted longer than the previous nine months in the field.

Then "the day" finally came in January of 1968 and I found myself boarding the stairs to the airplane that would take me back to sanity. I couldn't believe that I was finally getting out of there.

As the airplane clawed its way into the air for the long flight home, my thoughts raced back to my friends in Two-Nine. The night of the human wave attacks at Cam Lo, the lieutenant who wanted photos of his missing legs, the aborted attack on Hill 37, the five-hundred-pound bomb and forty wounded Marines, the ghostland of the DMZ . . .

Then the pictures that flashed into my consciousness

faded—replaced by one: the face of Lieutenant Carson. He smiled at me, and I could hear his voice deep inside.

"You okay, Doc? Don't sweat it, Doc. I _told_ you I'd take care of you."

I settled back in my seat, closed my eyes and whispered in answer: "I'm fine, sir. Just fine. And . . . thanks."

10

The DMZ

From the beginning, the Marines had opposed the construction of the "McNamara Line" and the supporting fire bases along the DMZ. To the Marines, who had always been an aggressively mobile, attack-oriented force, establishment of a permanent string of static outposts seemed a blunder. They felt it would tie down too many troops, be a logistical nightmare and would place them in easily located immobile targets. As it happened, they were right. The fire bases along Route 9 frequently came under long-range attack from across the "Z."

Positioned in well-camouflaged positions north of the Ben Hai River were pockets of heavy Chinese-made M-46 130 millimeter gun-howitzers capable of firing over 27,000 meters. This capability brought the Marine bases well within range of their deadly projectiles. To counter and knock out these big guns took a concerted effort by the Marines. The NVA gunners, limitations of the Marines' M-109 155mm self-propelled howitzers known, positioned their M-46s just out of range of counterbattery fire. The Marines became so frustrated at their inability to strike back that on several occasions B-52 strikes were called in to eliminate just one gun.

But they couldn't get them all. The Marines in the Fire Support Bases (FSBs) were safe neither day nor night. At any time, without warning, a rain of incoming rounds could strike, leaving death and destruction in its wake. And with each bombardment, the leathernecks suffered casualties.

Like their counterparts serving with the infantry companies, the corpsmen attached to the artillery units along Route 9 continually witnessed the carnage of war. HM3 Douglas Wean was attached to Kilo Battery, 4th Battalion, 12th Marines, a 155mm self-propelled artillery battery that moved with the infantry companies to wherever they were needed. He describes some of the injuries that artillery corpsmen encountered:

"The NVA artillery across the border did everything they could to silence our guns. Because of this, we had more shrapnel wounds than bullet wounds. But the very nature of the cannon gunners' jobs made them susceptible to on-the-job injuries that differed from those of the grunts. I had several hand wounds—lacerations incurred from working with the ammo cases, handling the cannisters, and getting caught in various pieces of machinery around the guns. Everything from loading trays to breechblocks had to be handled and moved. Guys were often getting their hands and fingers caught when they were rushing to get rounds downrange.

"I also had burns to treat. When you are 'firing for effect,' things get hot. And when you get hit by enemy artillery, things catch fire and burn. Explosions scorch skin if you are too close to them, and if they hit your ammo dump, well, it just keeps going and going and people get burned. Burns that are bad are not a pretty sight."

Wean elaborates on his unit's mission:

"There were two basic types of units along the 'Z'—grunts and artillery. The grunts did the sweeps and patrols, held the combat bases and pulled the recons. But they often got in over their heads. When they did, they needed some heavy-duty fire support. We provided that.

"Sure, the B-Fifty-Twos could plow up several acres of

ground on one strike, but they had to come from Guam. All of their missions had to be preplanned. Fighter-bombers were not always available, and when they were, they had to come from as far away as Da Nang or some aircraft carrier far out at sea. We were always there, just a radio call away. Within minutes, we could have steel on target."

For the corpsmen and the medics working in the fire bases, field medicine often became reminiscent of the Wild West days of the American frontier when doctors within the cavalry forts dealt with primitive conditions on a daily basis. Dirt floors, contaminated water, no electricity, crude working conditions and never enough medical supplies plagued the medical personnel of both eras. Col. William H. Arthur, an army surgeon assigned to Fort Washakie, Wyoming, as a young doctor in the 1870s wrote of one instance in dealing with a wounded trooper under similar conditions:

A cavalry soldier was accidentally shot in the right thigh, anterior aspect, upper third. The bullet passed across the limb in front of the femur, but tore through the femoral artery and it was necessary to tie the external iliac just below poupart's ligament. This operation was done in the ward on a mess table borrowed from one of the troop barracks, for our three attendants ate in the kitchen and we had no mess tables. Collateral circulation was not established and soon it was evident that gangrene of the foot and leg was inevitable. While waiting for a line of "demarcation" to form between the dead and viable tissues, I was called to the hospital one night to find that secondary hemorrhage had set in. The only chance it seemed to me of saving the man's life was amputation at the hip joint.

At night, by the light of a few candles, the operation was done. The anesthetic was given by the hospital cook, a private of cavalry. The hospital steward, recently appointed, fainted at the first stab of the knife, was shoved under a bed and left to come to in his own good time. A patient in the ward, a cavalry private, crawled out of bed, told me he had worked in a drugstore before enlisting and offered to help, and he did very well, and

66

the disarticulation was soon completed. The patient died before daybreak.

Almost a hundred years later, "Doc" Wean would find himself working under similar conditions. A fire base near the "Z" was essentially a frontier fort—and the Indians were everywhere.

11

HM3 Douglas L. Wean
Kilo Battery, 4th Battalion
12th Marines
Quang Tri Province, 1968

I never tried to be a hero. I only strived to do my job as well as I could. The real heroes, in my book, were guys like the young Marine who staggered into my sick bay bunker one morning about two-thirty.

Our battery's 155s had been firing for several minutes in support of a group of Marines under attack on Mutter's Ridge, a spine of hills paralleling the DMZ to our north. They were completely surrounded, were being hit badly, and in desperate need of all the support our howitzers could give. The night outside was strobed by the muzzle flashes of the big guns and my eardrums vibrated with the deep cough of each shot being fired.

"Doc, we have a wounded man here," said a Marine as he entered the confines of my small bunker, supporting another whose face grimaced in pain. "Can you do anything for him?"

I checked his wound. The back of his hand had been deeply lacerated and he was bleeding badly. He needed sutures—lots of them. The wound was so deep that I had to use a "baseball" suture to pull the wound margins together. The procedure was complicated by having to work under the glow of a Coleman lantern with equipment sterilized in a coffeepot, so I confined my treatment to just sewing him up as best I could. Anything more would have to wait until I could evacuate him to Dong Ha the next day for proper surgery and X-rays. I examined my work. It would hold until morning. I then wrapped his hand in gauze.

"That's it for tonight. Go to your bunker, get in the rack and try to keep your hand elevated. I'll get you out of here and down to Dong Ha tomorrow."

"Okay. Thanks, Doc."

I watched as he faded into the thunderous night.

Within an hour he was back. The bandages were gone, and his hand was ripped open again. I was furious. I knew that he had been "hand-ramming," a technique cannoneers use to bypass the hydraulic rammer to increase their rate of fire, sometimes not clearing their hand from the breech before the breechblock closed.

"What in the hell did you do?" I demanded.

"Doc, I had to go back to my gun. I'm a loader and I had to be at my station."

"Why?" I asked, impressed at his dedication but irritated that my previous work was for nothing.

"Doc, anytime there are Marines dying, and they are calling for our rounds, I've got to be at that gun. Those are *my* Marines out there."

I sewed him up again, wrapped the wound and sent him back to his gun.

"I understand," I mumbled after him. And I *did* understand. They were *my* Marines too. In no other branch of the service were there such feelings of comradeship and *esprit de corps* as in the Marine Corps. Even though I was navy, as an FMF corpsman I shared this strong feeling of dedication and loyalty. Loyalty in the corps is distributed to four entities in descending order: To God, To My Country, To My Corps, and To My Fellow Marines.

And now I was part of it. It was ironic because I had never planned it this way. When I enlisted in the navy, it was to *avoid* such a place as this. Yet, no matter what I did, some invisible force directed my fate back to a path that led to Quang Tri Province. After the young Marine returned to his gun, I sat down in a reflective mood and listened to the cannon fire. I began thinking of the things that had happened to me that led up to my current situation. I had witnessed and participated in things that I had never even dreamed of two years before when I was a draft-age, eighteen-year-old kid still in high school.

The *draft*. That terrifying word that represented a mechanism that could reach out and grab you, no matter where you were or what you were doing, and mold you into a cog for the "green machine." Once constructed, you were then transported thousands of miles away to kill or be killed by people you never knew existed. When the word *draft* entered my mind, it was synonymous with the word *army*. Army meant ground warfare. Boots. Packs. Rifles. Heat. That wasn't a place I wanted to be. In March 1966 I turned eighteen and registered. I knew that within the next few months the inevitable envelope from Uncle Sam would come, and unless I figured out how to beat the system, I'd soon be wearing boots and carrying a pack—in *Vietnam*.

"We'll have to get you enlisted in the navy so you can ride a ship and avoid that Vietnam war," my father counseled after hearing my concerns. "You're from a *navy* family, son. I did my part in the South Pacific in the Second World War as a gunner's mate and your older brother spent his time at Newport, Rhode Island, as a presidential staff driver for Eisenhower. Now it's time to do your part but that doesn't mean you have to go to Vietnam. Those Vietcong can't get you in the navy."

August 1966 found me in boot camp at the Naval Training Center at Great Lakes, Illinois. When I graduated three months later, I was given a book to look at that had the Military Occupational Skills—known as MOS's—and told to pick one. Whatever I picked would be my job, and possibly my career, during my stay in the navy. I was given fifteen minutes to make up my mind. I studied the book intensely, turning pages as fast as I could. *A ship! Look for something on a ship!*

On one page was a photograph of a sailor wearing a white doctor's coat and looking through a microscope. That looked interesting. I looked at the designation: Hospital Corpsman. That was for me. A hospital corpsman—aboard a *ship.*

I didn't have to go far. The school was right there at Great Lakes. In the twenty-one weeks we spent in training, we learned the things that would be needed by a corpsman expected to function in a hospital ward, a sick bay of a ship at sea, or in a clinic. But because we might find ourselves working far from outside support, such as those who would be assigned to a ship at sea, we received very detailed training. It was during one of these classes, as I sat daydreaming about sailing into some far-off exotic port, that I was brought back to reality by the lights being turned off. The movie screen had been pulled down and it drew my attention as the countdown numbers of a typical military training film flashed on it. I watched with halfhearted interest, thinking that here was another boring film about splints or bandaging or how to cut out an ingrown toenail. But this film was different.

"This was Korea," said the instructor, pointing at the screen where soldiers appeared to be huddling over other wounded soldiers. What did this have to do with us?

"These are field corpsmen assigned to the Marine Corps working in actual combat conditions on the battlefield. Since the navy provides all medical services to the Marines, some of you will probably see service wearing the green uniform of a grunt."

I didn't like the sound of that. And the situation didn't appear to improve later as we gathered at the barracks.

"Those of you who do not garner good grades will probably be sent to the Marines," warned my company commander. We had no reason to doubt him.

I studied hard and graduated in the top 10 percent of my class. But then, as fate often has its diverse ways of reversing circumstances, the needs of the navy dictated that all those on my class roster with last names beginning with the letters *A* through *M* would be sent to other navy schools for further education. The rest were assigned to the Marines Corps. Visions of combat boots and green uniforms filled my head as I packed my seabag for Camp Lejeune.

Montford Point, the Field Medical Service School located at Lejeune, gave us training in field combat medicine and all the unique aspects of supporting and working with the Marines in the field. This additional training included weapons and tactics. *Weapons* and *tactics*—two words that never entered my mind when I saw that photo of the guy wearing the lab coat in the MOS book.

A stint in the naval hospital at Portsmouth, Virginia was followed by orders to Okinawa for further field training and finally orders for Vietnam. By this time I expected it and was almost relieved when they came. At least the waiting was over.

Then, like a partial reprieve from hell, I discovered that instead of a grunt outfit, I was being assigned to an artillery battalion. At least I wouldn't be *walking* everywhere—and surely it had to be much safer. I headed for Camp J. J. Carroll feeling that my tour in Vietnam wouldn't be so bad after all.

The fire base was located in the far northern Quang Tri Province near the demilitarized zone bordering North Vietnam. Upon arrival, I surveyed my surroundings. The camp was located in the open, surrounded by the steep, green ridges and rain forests of the Annamite Mountains, halfway between Con Thien and Khe Sanh. Not a good place to be in 1968. When I reported to the CO, I found out just how bad things were. When you are briefed by Marines, they don't pull any punches.

"Doc, here's the scoop," said Capt. Hal Sullivan, Kilo Battery's commander, as he motioned me to a seat in the command bunker. "We're an M-109 self-propelled howitzer battery. The 109 is a 155 millimeter gun that can fire a ninety-eight-pound projectile 14,600 meters—about nine miles—with incredible accuracy. The problem around here is that the NVA have those big Russian and Chinese 152 millimeter jobs that can shoot almost *eleven* miles, and even worse, 130 millimeter field guns that lob rounds up to 31,000 meters. That means they can hit us but we can't hit them. And they got somewhere over a hundred and thirty of them north of the Ben Hai River aimed at the various Marine outposts along the 'Z.' We don't know how many are sighted in on us here, but in a duel we could come up on the short end of the stick with our six guns.

"Now I've got one hundred and thirty-four Marines and five officers in this battery. They're *my* Marines, but *you* are responsible for the health and medical care of every one of them. As battery corpsman, you're also responsible for a few other pleasant jobs, such as dispensing malaria and salt pills, emplacing piss tubes, burning out the shitters, and killin' rats. And we definitely got a rat problem. Welcome to Vietnam, Doc."

As I lugged my gear through the scorching heat to my bunker, I surveyed the area. Camp Carroll, which faintly reminded me of a frontier fort in the Old West, was surrounded by coils of concertina barbed wire, interspersed with both claymore and land mines. Behind the wire were sandbagged bunkers and wooden watchtowers. Within the perimeter, dug into the red dirt of Quang Tri Province, were gun pits where the green snouts of the 155s projected into the sky like patient guard dogs waiting for the order to attack. With these big guns and the local line company Marines to protect me, what did I have to fear inside the safe appearance of this fire base? But then, there *were* those Russian and Chinese guns the Skipper mentioned . . .

Within two days I found that Captain Sullivan hadn't exaggerated about the rats. The bastards were everywhere. They bred under the shitter, in empty ammo cases, and anywhere else they could hide. Nothing in the compound was safe from their nocturnal raids. They bit sleeping Marines, chewed through canvas and wooden cases, and ate anything they could swallow. Within the main frame of this war of men was another, more personal war taking place within the wire-strung perimeter of Camp Carroll—a war declared by rodents.

I was called to the CP bunker.

"Doc, you've got to get a handle on these rats. They've

taken over the whole goddamned area. I don't like it when they effect the health and morale of *my* Marines. See what you can do—whatever it takes," ordered Kilo's Gunny. I could tell that he was really pissed at the rat situation.

There it was again. The word *my*. First they were the Skipper's Marines, then they were the Gunny's. It seemed like a big family where everyone claimed to be the father.

I did some checking around and a bit of research and found that a chemical known as warfarin sodium was supposed to cause internal hemorrhaging in animals that swallowed the stuff. It appeared that it would make a suitable poison, but how would I get the rats to eat it?

Then it came to me. Like mice, rats love peanut butter. In many of the C ration meals were small tins of ancient peanut butter graciously provided by some bygone civilian vendor. I opened dozens of cans and spent hours mixing peanut butter with the chemicals, then forming the awful stuff into little balls that I could sprinkle around the infested areas. Sure enough, the rats loved it and within a few days the rodent population began to decrease. I felt rather pleased with myself. The Skipper would be happy, the Gunny would be happy, and I would be a local hero. But I didn't know about the side effects of the poison. Two days later I found out.

"Doc, you better come and take a look at this," said a frantic Marine who framed the open "hatch" of my bunker.

"What's up?" I asked, wondering if someone had been injured and I would need my Unit One—my trusty aid bag.

"You just better come. Ya gotta see it for yourself," he replied as he motioned for me to follow.

I trailed him across the compound until we came to the suspended lister bag, a large canvas sack filled with water and surrounded at the bottom by plastic faucets—where we all filled our canteens. Several bare-chested Marines milled around, staring at me disgustedly.

"Look inside," said the young Marine, wrinkling his nose.

I stood on an ammo crate and peered over the edge. I did not know when I concocted the poison mixture that the first symptom in the victim was an overwhelming thirst—and this lister bag was the nearest water. Inside floated over a hundred of the filthy animals. The bag was packed.

"Wonder how many guys filled their canteens before we found the rats?" asked the Marine, looking a bit squeamish.

I looked at him in horror, imagining some poor guy turning a canteen up for a long swig. I stepped down, told the spectators to empty and clean the lister bag, mumbled something about a recall notice on all canteens in the camp and began making plans to counter the wrath of the Skipper and the Gunny—and the next world outbreak of bubonic plague.

Camp Carroll was our main base, but we didn't always stay there. As a self-propelled howitzer battery, our guns were mounted on tracks much like a tank and could go just about anywhere. When the line battalions moved, so did we. If they needed our heavy firepower to support them, we were there. The coming weeks would find me applying my medical training on operations in such places as fire bases Charlie One, Two, and Three—which covered the eastern quarter of the demilitarized zone—the Rockpile, Mai Loc and firebase Alpha Three near Con Thien. At the time, I didn't realize how these names would be burned into American history. They were just names. But names become more important after blood is shed there.

The heat of August bore down on us as we set up in Delta Five, the combat zone south of Mai Loc in the Ba Long Valley. We had been requested to bring three guns up to provide fire support for some Marine line companies working the area. We had set up a temporary fire base, emplaced the guns and built bunkers. Everything went well for the first couple of days. Then the demon of bad luck joined us.

The morning of August 5 dawned bright and I had just started to brew some C ration coffee when I heard the crack of an explosion echo just outside our small perimeter. I jerked my head in the direction of the sound and could see a black cloud billowing into the air, changing shape as it caught the wind currents.

Orders were shouted within the compound and a platoon

was hastily formed to investigate the blast. Whatever it was, it had occurred on or near the supply road that our trucks used every day. I felt I knew what had happened. I prayed I was wrong.

I wasn't. We hadn't gone far when we discovered what was left of one of our supply trucks. It now lay beside the road as twisted, smoking wreckage, victim of a large Russian mine. The driver had been blown through the canvas top of the cab and was lying on the side of the road. The platoon quickly formed a perimeter to provide security while I ran toward the victim.

When I got to him I could see that he had an open fracture of the upper arm and several compound fractures of the lower arm and elbow. Bright red blood from shattered arteries pumped onto the dirt in rapid spurts, adding a deeper redness to the clay.

I recognized him immediately: Cpl. Jimmy Bryant, an easygoing guy and a good friend to everyone who met him—including me. He looked up into my eyes as I knelt at his side and began working on him.

"You ain't gonna medevac me, are ya, Doc?"

"I sure am, Jimmy. It's pretty much the end of your war. You're going home."

"Doc, ya can't do that. Ya gotta fix me up so I can stay."

Must be shock setting in, I thought, *obviously he doesn't know what he's saying.* "You've done all you can do here, Jimmy. It's time to go home."

"But you don't understand, Doc. My battery needs me. I gotta drive the roads to bring up rounds. If I don't deliver, they can't fire their missions. They all depend on me. I gotta take care of my guys."

My. That word again. At first I hadn't really understood. What was it that brought men so close together that they would do anything—including die—for their fellows? Now I was beginning to understand. It wasn't any one thing, it was a combination of several factors that all meld together to form a bond stronger than steel. The war, the terror, the dying, and every other unspeakable horror men face in combat is countered by a combination of comradeship, trust, dedication, an ingrained instinct for survival, and in the Marine Corps, history and tradition. These guys weren't only responsible to each other, but to all the Marines who had come before. It was a family where one generation followed another and each passed a code of honor to the next. It wasn't really patriotism or loyalty to a higher authority, it was a sense of responsibility to fellow Marines —past and present. Everybody felt like they were an important part of the family, or the team. They were made to feel that way. A feeling of need built dedication, and dedication built pride. Nowhere at home, or anywhere else in life, did a man feel as needed by his friends as he did here. It was all beginning to make sense. And I was beginning to feel a part of it. They made me feel needed and important too. I was part of the team. I was *the* Doc.

It wasn't always firefights and blood-and-guts. Combat— moments of high intensity fighting, killing and dying—are punctuation marks to the daily life of warfare. The paragraphs are the things that happen in the day-to-day activities of a combat unit composed by young men far from home living on the edge of terror and death. A corpsman in a combat zone, much like his brethren aboard a ship far at sea, has myriad duties that involve the welfare of his charges. The captain may be in charge of their activities and discipline, the chaplain their souls, but the corpsmen were in charge of a lot in between—their health, and often times, their complete well-being. It was on such an occasion that I had to become an instant psychiatrist who officed in a sandbagged bunker. The nearest doctor was at regimental headquarters at Dong Ha about twenty miles away. In Camp Carroll, *I* was the doctor—and the doctor was always in.

"Doc? The Skipper said for me to see you."

I turned and was greeted by the sight of a young eighteen-year-old Marine with a disturbed look. He seemed young to me, after all, I was by then an ancient twenty. An old man.

"What's the problem?" I asked, motioning him to a seat on an upturned ammo crate.

"Well, I got this here letter. It's from my girlfriend. Seems she don't want to wait for me to come home. She ain't even sure I *am* coming home. And now she's found someone else, some shitbird 'Jody' puke to take my place. It just ain't worth livin' now, Doc. I've thought about just killin' myself. After all, why wait for Charlie to do it?"

I listened intently, pursed my lips, thought with a display of reflective looks, then offered advice. Hell, I didn't even *have* a girlfriend. I didn't have that much experience, at least not enough to be a counselor, but I was the only one around he could turn to. I told him several things, but above all I told him how valuable he was to the battery and to the other Marines who depended on him—*his* Marines. It seemed to work and he appeared a lot less distressed when he left. I felt better too. He was another one of *my* Marines, and I was *his* Doc.

My garrison duties at Camp Carroll were continually fragmented by excursions with the battery to the other combat bases within the province. Like the rats of Camp Carroll, the rats of Vietnam—the 324-B NVA Regiment, the first disciplined regulars to take the Marines on in strength —plagued us throughout our Tactical Area of Responsibility, or TAOR, as the Marines called it.

We constantly traded punches. Their guns versus our guns. In June we had succeeded in knocking out two of the elusive 130mm guns north of the DMZ, then when we moved to Con Thien, the radio crackled when an air observer spotted a reinforced NVA company moving toward Gio Linh, approximately five miles northeast of us.

Marines sprang to action. It was an artillery battery's dream—enemy troops in the open, in broad daylight, with *six* howitzers in range! Then the command came: *Battery adjust!*

We set a battalion record that day. Within ninety minutes the battery fired 410 rounds, and by the end of the fire mission, eleven hours later, we had expended 1,118 rounds. A lot of NVA died that day. And for this action we became a marked unit by the 324-B Regiment. They wanted our blood. Then after reorganizing, like the rats of Camp Carroll, they came back hungry. And one of the worst infected areas was a place called the Rockpile.

The first week in September found me traveling with half of our battery—three guns—to two steep and rocky crags that jutted skyward like huge upright volcanic tits. Though the Vietnamese named the twin mountains "The Wings of Angels," one look at the gigantic monoliths revealed why the Marines called this place the Rockpile. Their seven-hundred-foot elevation commanded the surrounding area, making the Rockpile a tactical imperative to control of the upper Cam Lo River Valley and its rugged multilayered canopy jungle and coarse razor and elephant grass.

Many fierce battles had occurred around these peaks. They were the highest ground in the area and commanded the surrounding terrain with natural majesty. Both the North Vietnamese Army and the U.S. Marines wanted it, and neither hesitated in putting up a fight for it.

No sooner had we arrived than the sporadic crack of small arms fire and the whooping whistle of mortar and artillery rounds began to make the 324-B's presence known in the vicinity. On the second day, they engaged a unit of the 9th Marines just northeast of us, and finally withdrew leaving twenty-one bodies behind. At 0815 on September 2, the command *Battery Adjust* echoed through the air, sending Marine gun crews running to their weapons. The following action was entered into the log:

020815—"K" fired 93 HE danger close defensive fires for Recon Team Badminton at 035642 resulting in 50 possible KIA's. (Team stated that "arms and legs flew into the air" but unable to give confirmed body count— figure not included in totals for casualties inflicted.)

Nine days later, thirty-four NVA were killed during a fierce firefight just northwest of our positions, and only a week after that, on September 17, a Marine rifle company came under intense mortar and heavy artillery fire nearby, losing twenty-five killed and 126 wounded. We supported each contact with our big guns, and each contact grew closer to our positions. It was like the NVA were slowly tightening a noose.

The next day we moved the guns to support elements of the 3rd, 9th, and 26th Marine Regiments, operating near the Rockpile against our old nemesis, and were in position by dark. The next day was uneventful, other than sporadic flurries of activity on the radio and the occasional small arms fire. But the air seemed to thicken with an electric sense of anticipation. Then a message from Hanoi came to us by way of "Hanoi Hannah," the English-speaking North Vietnamese propaganda announcer, on our transistor radios.

". . . And for the Marines, you really should not have moved that platoon from K Battery, 4th Battalion, 12th Marines to what you call the Rockpile. You will pay for your trip from Camp Carroll with blood." Old "Gloom-and-Doom" Hannah knew who we were and where we had come from, undoubtedly informed by the 324-B. Maybe it was just talk. It often was.

I woke up on the morning of the 19th thinking of the success of making it through another night in Vietnam. But that day would prove that the night was not the only dangerous time.

About ten-thirty I heard the first distinct *pop* of mortar rounds, followed within seconds by the scream of incoming 122 millimeter rockets. This was joined by the crackle of AK-47 and machine-gun fire coming from the perimeter. I dove for cover.

I couldn't believe it. They were attacking in broad daylight. We had experienced nightly incoming fire and probes, but nothing in the daytime. First, the attacks grew closer to the Rockpile with every contact, now an attack in the light of day!

The first few rounds created chaos. Troops scurried toward the nearest cover as the incoming projectiles impacted within the perimeter, spewing geysers of dirt and rock into the air. Three thoughts exploded in my mind like a task list for survival: Weapon, Cover, and Keep My Head Down.

I dove toward my hole just as a 122 millimeter rocket hit ten yards away, sending shrapnel into my left jaw and slamming my head to the right with a violent jerk. I fell to the bottom of the hole in a daze. When my wits returned, I could see blood on my right hand, which had been lacerated by fragments from the exploding rocket. But before I could react to my own wounds, the world exploded over me in a thunderous shock wave as our ammo dump took a direct hit. Powder canisters and 155 millimeter projectiles, along with various explosives, grenades and small arms ammo, exploded in a chain of ignitions. I crawled to the edge of my hole and peered over. A huge black mushroom cloud blocked out the sun as it rolled skyward. The fire that drove the smoke was intense. Heat could be felt all the way across to my position. I stared, momentarily stunned at the violence of activity, when I was brought to reality by the screams of wounded and the shouts of "Doc! Where's the Doc? Get the Doc!"

These words are every corpsman and medic's fear. But these were Marines—*my* Marines. They were *my* responsibility. I grabbed my bag and ran toward the shouting.

Lance Cpl. Hector "Dino" Rivera was the first man I found. He had been blown into the air and was lying about ten feet from a burning bunker. I slid to his side, tearing my bag open as I evaluated his wounds. It was bad. His left foot had been almost severed at the ankle and was completely turned around, hanging by nothing more than the Achilles tendon. Farther up, bright red arterial blood pumped in spurts from his calf. This was dangerous. Arterial blood, the blood carrying oxygen to the organs of the body, is bright red. When an artery is severed, the blood shoots out of a wound in spurts with each beat of the heart. The victim will rapidly bleed to death unless it is quickly stopped.

As fast as I could I strapped and tightened a tourniquet below his knee, then reached down and gently turned his foot around. Something had to be done to the wound with its mutilated ankle socket. I tore open a large battle dressing and packed the wound to stop the remaining blood flow. Finally winding it tight with an Ace wrap, I looked at Dino's face to see how he was doing.

Dino looked up. "Am I going to die, Doc?"

I could see apprehension and fear in his eyes. He knew he was in bad shape, but did not realize how serious he really was. He trusted my judgment and needed to know.

"No, you're going home," I reassured him, showing my best poker face. What else could I say? I always used that line. It worked to combat trauma and shock, gave the casualty something to look forward to. But before I could reinforce this statement the situation worsened.

More explosions blasted earth into the air around us. Incoming fire continued to pour in, giving no respite to the beleaguered garrison. I couldn't move. We were caught in the open and any attempt to stand up to get Rivera out of there would mean instant death from flying shrapnel.

The ammo dump continued to erupt in balls of fire, sending even more debris and shrapnel sailing through the air, joining that of the steel made in Russia. I hunkered down over Rivera, shielding him as well as I could. He was one of *my* Marines, and he needed me. My job was to save lives, and by God that was what I was going to do. I was beginning to feel frustrated and angry. Dino didn't have a flak jacket on, and the only way I could protect him until I could drag him to safety was to shield him from harm by lying over his body.

As I did this, explosion followed explosion, wounding me several more times. Finally, there was a slight reprieve in hell as the incoming fire momentarily slackened. I thought I might be able to pull Dino to the safety of a nearby shell crater if I hurried. I grabbed his good ankle and began dragging him. After what seemed like an eternity, we reached the crater and I pulled him inside as quickly and gently as possible. But I couldn't stop there. There were many more wounded Marines to attend to, still trapped outside on the smoke-covered battleground. As a squad of Marines crawled up and took charge of Dino, I slid out of the crater and again made my way across the impact zone toward the bunker area.

I located another wounded Marine, Private, First Class Cauthen, who was lying on his stomach suffering from multiple wounds in his back, buttocks and legs. I checked him quickly. There was no arterial bleeding, but he obviously had a concussion and was in shock. Shock is a killer. If I couldn't bring him around, even though the wounds didn't look immediately life threatening, he could die from shock. I grabbed him and started slapping him about, screaming at him to wake up and pay attention. When he came around I began shielding him with my body as I had Dino, for shrapnel still filled the air with its deadly song. At the first opportunity, I grabbed both of his legs and began dragging him backward toward safety, sliding him on his belly. As I struggled with Cauthen, several more artillery and rocket rounds struck the ground around me, each time knocking me down. I had only one thought: Get back up and get Cauthen out of here.

We finally made it to the safety of a shell crater. I worked on him and got him stabilized. After he was taken care of I worked on five more wounded Marines that had been brought to me, then arranged for evacuation as needed. After the last man was treated I began to take stock of my own condition. As I poked and probed my body I discovered that I had been hit by shrapnel in the left side of my jaw, right hand, both buttocks, lower back, and suffered powder burns all over my upper back.

I made my way to the local BAS (Battalion Aid Station) and was treated by another corpsman working there. He wanted to medevac me, but I couldn't go.

I couldn't leave the battery. They needed me. I was their "Doc," and they were *my* Marines.

For conspicuous gallantry in action on September 19, 1968, while under an intensive artillery barrage from North Vietnamese Artillery, PO Douglas L. Wean was awarded the Silver Star.

12

The River War

Monsoon season brings great billowing clouds rushing in from the South China Sea like angry beasts in search of prey. As they build overhead, a dark misty grayness covers the land. When the rain begins, it falls in cold driving sheets that pound the jungles, mountains, valleys and rice fields until every stream, every canal, every river swells until their banks can no longer contain the torrential downpour. It is during this time that the actions of men and machines bog down in submission to the elements. In some areas, the only operations that can be conducted are those accomplished by boat.

When monsoon season ends, the water recedes until it is once again contained within the river and stream banks. But even in the dry season, Vietnam remains a country laced by rivers of sufficient size to permit navigation by boat and amphibious vehicles. Not only were the rivers used as a means of transporting combat troops, conducting waterborne patrols and penetrating communist strongholds, but were often critical as a means of transporting supplies in volume that couldn't be handled by helicopter.

The importance of these waterways did not escape the NVA and VC. Great efforts were expended to interdict the use of these vital supply lines by the use of ambushes, man-made obstacles and mines. For those traveling the rivers, the twisting ribbons held constant danger.

American ingenuity quickly targeted on the river war. In the Delta, high-speed PBR Swift Boats, drawing no more than a few inches of water, patrolled the main channel and tributaries of the Mekong. Infantry units were transported into battle on specialized armored landing crafts, while Monitors—armored riverboats—mounting both heavy machine guns and flamethrowers, escorted the infantry to protect them from riverbank ambushes.

In the north, the Dong Ha, Cam Lo, and Cua Viet rivers snake their way inland from the coast at Cua Viet toward the Marine fire support bases that guarded the DMZ. While it was the navy's responsibility to patrol this vital lifeline and transport the supplies needed by the FSBs (Fire Support Bases), the task of providing amphibious vehicles fell to the Marine amphibious tractor battalions. Known as "amtracs," these tracked troop carriers were equally at home in the water and on land. Duty with the amtrac companies was a unique experience to the corpsmen who found themselves attached to them. And like their brethren that served with the infantry units who daily faced death at every turn of the trail, the corpsmen who worked the river found danger lurking around every bend. For like the rivers of the south, the Dong Ha, Cam Lo, and Cua Viet rivers became a target for the North Vietnamese.

Hospital Corpsman Lyle Wells never envisioned going to Vietnam—or being assigned to the Marines—when he volunteered to become a corpsman. It wasn't until his class was in its final weeks of training at the Naval Hospital in San Diego that he was to find out that corpsmen did other things besides work in a hospital.

"The first indication I had that navy corpsmen served with the Marines was when a petty officer walked into our classroom one day and announced that my entire class had been selected for Field Medical School at Camp Pendleton.

I wasn't sure what that meant, but when he told us, I was shocked.

"I had joined the Naval Reserve because my father couldn't afford to send both me and my sister to college, and she was already there. That only left one place for me to go after graduation from high school: the service. I didn't want to get drafted and serve in the infantry so I joined the Navy Reserve on the Delayed Entry Program just before my senior year. My two-week Christmas break was spent in San Diego training to become a fireman, a sailor who works in the engine room of a ship. We had all heard how hot and dirty this job was and I wasn't thrilled at the prospect of spending my two years of active duty confined to such a miserable place.

"When one of the instructors announced that there were five slots for corpsmen, and explained what a corpsman was, I jumped at the chance. Working in a clean hospital or in the sick bay of a ship was a prospect I couldn't pass up. At least it would keep me out of the engine room.

"But he never said anything about the Marines.

"After four weeks of humping the hills of Camp Pendleton and learning all the weapons and field skills needed by an FMF (Fleet Marine Force) corpsman, a horrible feeling descended over the class. The navy wasn't putting us through all this unless we were going to Vietnam. But after graduation, months passed as we worked in the wards in the hospital back at San Diego and we all began breathing a sigh of relief. When July of 1968 came, we all knew that they couldn't fit a twelve-month tour in WestPac into the nine months of active duty that remained on our reserve commitment. We were wrong.

"We threw a big party to celebrate beating the system. Had we known that at that very moment we were all being extended, there would have been no revelry. In September the orders came. They read like a roster for a class reunion. We were all going to the 3rd Marine Division.

"We all knew where that meant. Vietnam. And we all knew that the 3rd was FMF, and that meant infantry. I had had it pretty easy so far, but now my luck had run out. At least that's what I thought when we boarded the plane at Travis Air Force Base for Okinawa.

"Two weeks later I stood in a long line of corpsmen waiting for assignments in a Quonset hut at Quang Tri. I could see a large status board on the wall behind a chief petty officer who sat behind a table busily handing out papers to those in line and then turning to add a name to an empty slot on the board. Most of the openings were under the heading '9th Marines.'

"As the line shuffled forward it appeared that all of the guys ahead of me who stepped to the chief's table turned away clutching slips that designated one of the battalions of the 9th.

"We all had heard about the 9th. They were infantry, and they took a lot of casualties. Their nickname was 'The Walking Dead.' Not very reassuring.

"When my turn came I reached for the slip of paper with trembling hands. I was afraid to even look down. When I finally did, the number nine stood out as if it were a neon sign. My heart sank.

"Just then, another chief came into the room and walked up to the table.

"'Hey, you said I could have two out of this bunch,' he said with irritation to the chief making the assignments. The seated chief looked up and shrugged. He looked at me and asked: 'You wanna go to amtracs?'

"'I don't know. What's amtracs?'

"'A lot better than where you're supposed to go now, believe me.'

"I looked at the big number nine scrawled on my slip. 'Sure. I'll go to amtracs.'

"I wasn't sure, but I felt that maybe my luck was beginning to change."

13

HM3 Lyle W. Wells
1st Amtrac Battalion
3rd Marine Division
Cua Viet, Quang Tri Province,
1968

My luck had not only been good, it had been incredible. Instead of an infantry unit—the FMF—I had received orders for amtracs. Instead of walking, if I had to go anywhere, I'd be riding. At least that's what I thought when I reported in to the 1st Amphibious Tractor Battalion at Cua Viet.

Cua Viet was on the coast where the Dong Ha River empties into the South China Sea. Besides the amtrac battalion, the facility contained a large navy base with all the amenities afforded the navy anywhere in the world, including excellent chow and duties that were almost the same as we had in the States. Then to cap it all off, on the east end of camp was a beautiful white sand beach where we could spend off-duty hours floating in the surf on rubber mattresses to while away the time and wait for our tours to end.

In stark contrast to the navy side, the Marine amtrac battalion had its own compound that was more what one would expect in a war zone. Overlooking the Dong Ha River, the compound was a dug-in installation set up in a defensive posture with watchtowers, concertina wire, trenches and bunkers. These bunkers weren't average sand-bagged holes, but were the best bunkers in the country—buried derelict amtracs capable of withstanding direct hits from just about anything the gooks had to throw at them.

In the center of all this was a large steel tower used by the Naval Gunfire Liaison Officer to call counterbattery fire against the big North Vietnamese artillery pieces across the DMZ a little over a mile and a half away. With the border of North Vietnam so close, incoming rounds from across the border hit Cua Viet almost daily. But the NVA were very cautious when they shot because our reply could be sixteen-inch naval gunfire from the USS *New Jersey,* capable of striking up to twenty-eight miles inland and penetrating the most reinforced bunker. Because of this, the NVA gunners hid their cannons in caves, rolled them out to fire a few shots, then quickly rolled them back in before we could fire counterbattery. It was the job of the ANGLICO (Air and Naval Gunfire Liaison Company) officer in the tower to locate the muzzle flashes across the border and call in fire from the ships to silence the enemy efforts. We corpsmen considered this great sport. When incoming rounds began to fall, the first corpsman to get to the ladder to the tower could go up and watch the officer as he directed the big naval guns offshore. And because the nature of bursting artillery rounds caused shrapnel to follow paths near the ground, the tower was a very safe place to be during artillery duels.

Between the beach, the chow, the decent working hours, the daily incoming rounds that broke up the boredom, and the sport of watching it all from "The Tower," I couldn't help but think if this is Vietnam, it's great.

But I was soon to find there was more to Vietnam than this.

First Amtracs was charged with the security of the Dong Ha River from the South China Sea to five miles west of Dong Ha toward Cam Lo. This was an important function since the river was used as a daily pipeline for supplies and personnel traveling upriver. Boats of every size and description could be seen navigating the river, hauling troops, vehicles, ammunition and other necessary items of war to the Marine garrisons inland.

And because of this, the NVA developed a plan of attack to stem the flow of supplies. With large satchel-type mines strapped to their backs, sappers who were in extremely good physical shape ran on foot every night from their lairs across the border straight to the river, activated the mines and tossed them into the water to drift until an unwary vessel met them. Other NVA elements infiltrated the areas around Cua Viet to set up ambushes for the Marine patrols being conducted as security measures against the sappers. Then each morning, mine sweepers had to clear the river of mines before river traffic could commence for the day's routine.

Alpha and Bravo companies of the battalion patrolled on foot just like the grunt units. With each company was one of our corpsmen. About two o'clock in the afternoon, a patrol would leave the compound and go out about ten klicks, set up and watch for infiltrating NVA units and sappers. Then after return and a day off, the group would become the reactionary force, sleeping together in one building in case of call-out. Each of the twelve corpsmen assigned to the battalion rotated through these duties, with two being out with the companies at all times.

Even with the patrol duties, the daily artillery strikes, the NVA infiltrators and the mines in the river, Cua Viet didn't seem such a bad place to spend the war.

Until the ship hit the mine.

I had only been with Alpha Company about a week and had just returned to my hooch from passing out malaria pills to the troops when I heard what sounded like a muffled *whump!* come from the river. We looked in the direction of the sound in time to see a huge waterspout erupt under an

LCT (Landing Craft Tank) in midstream. The massive steel hull surged skyward, bent in the middle and fell back into the water. A cloud of mist hung over it like a burst of steam from a locomotive. We immediately knew there would be casualties.

"Grab your stuff and follow me," screamed a sergeant who came running up from the river. I snatched up a medical bag and joined the other corpsmen from the hooch as we fell into trail "on the double" behind the Marines. Boarding amtracs that quickly lurched and bumped toward the water's edge, we slid down the bank and entered the muddy water like huge green alligators on the prowl. Belching black diesel smoke skyward, the engine roared as it spun the tracks underwater that propelled us toward the smoking hulk. Even from our noisy perch on top of the 'trac, the screams of injured men could be heard drifting across the water.

As we drew close I began to realize what had happened. The ship had actually hit one of the mines I had heard about but had never witnessed. For the first time the realization that all the bullshit was over and there actually was a war going on and could cause very real casualties hit me. Up until then I had handled BAS sick calls, given a few shots, passed out pills and Band-Aids, but no real war-type injuries. That had just changed.

We pulled up near the bow of the boat and the first man I could see was a sailor who was desperately hanging on to a machine-gun mount to keep from falling. Both of his legs were compound fractures with bone sticking out of the skin. The hull of the LCT had been thrust up so violently from the explosion that his legs had virtually collapsed from bone failure. He wasn't the only one. Every man in the crew had almost identical fractures.

I jumped to the gunwale of the boat and climbed over. Each man I found needed splints and battle dressings to stop the flow of blood. Then I came to the wheelhouse. The crew all wore helmets and flak jackets, which normally would have protected them against shrapnel and head injuries. But those in the wheelhouse didn't stand a chance, even with the helmets.

The wheelhouse was very small, but four men had been inside when the boat hit the mine. Two of them wore helmets, but the force of the explosion had driven them into the overhead with such power that the helmets they wore were of little protection and had even been destroyed by the impact. The two that did not have helmets . . . well, in the wheelhouse there were no survivors.

By now the Marines had lined amtracs up from the wreck to the bank, tied side by side like a long pier. We began carrying off the wounded and the dead, walking across the backs of the tractors like a bridge. As we approached the bank, a large helicopter landed and a colonel got out.

"There's no medevac close, so use my chopper to get these people to Dong Ha. I can wait here until they're taken care of," said the colonel. We loaded the casualties and I watched as the machine lifted to a hover, casting great clouds of billowing dust over us, turned away and rose into the air. I had never seen a full colonel before. I spoke with him a few minutes after the helicopter had left and he seemed like a regular guy. He must have been, because he explained that he had overheard the call for medevac over the radio as he was flying and had canceled his trip to respond to our call for one reason—to save Marine lives. I was impressed.

We went back to our quarters and began refilling our expended aid bags. It had taken everything we carried to treat the casualties. As we worked I heard more boats coming up the river. I looked and could see minesweepers rounding the bend to begin their sweeps in an effort to locate any more of the infernal devices. The river would be closed until the sweepers had completed their search.

Five hours later the river was declared open. From around the bend came six smaller landing craft about the size of an LCM (Landing Craft Mechanized). As the first grew close I heard another, but smaller, *whump!*

I now knew what that sound meant. Again we raced for the amtracs. Drivers mounted, started the engines and closed the landing gates. Once more we entered the water.

We had farther to go this time. Finally we drew close to the crippled boat and could see what had happened. The boat had hit a smaller mine, causing damage to the bow. Several people wearing civilian clothes sat in the back relatively unharmed with the exception of bruises and contusions. Two others that were in the bow were less fortunate. The boat was carrying a civilian USO troupe on their way upriver to entertain the troops. A large black man, one of the USO troupers, had been sitting on the gunwale and had been blown completely out of the boat. He now floated facedown in the river.

With great difficulty—he weighed about 250 pounds—we fished him from the water and pulled him aboard one of the other boats that by now had tied up with the rest in a cluster. I examined the man and could see that he had a large swelling of the throat. Something had struck him across his trachea and massive swelling was cutting his air off. I began mouth-to-mouth resuscitation, working as quickly as I could in a frantic attempt to bring him around. But something was wrong.

"Bill, give it up," said another corpsman that was watching. "It's too late."

I ignored him and continued to work. I had to do everything I could. I was the doctor and he was my patient—and beyond that, he was a man who would die without my help. Then, almost when I was at the point of exhaustion, it dawned on me that his chest wasn't moving. I couldn't get air into his lungs due to the swelling of his throat. It was completely constricted.

"Come on, Bill. It's no good."

I felt for a pulse. There was none. He was right. There was nothing I could do. At least with the knowledge I had then, there was nothing I could do. Later I would learn about tracheotomies, but on that day the procedure was foreign to me. And other than a Swiss Army knife, we had nothing to do one with anyway.

I had seen too much for one day. Vietnam, the Vietnam I had feared, burst into my mind for the first time as the place of death and destruction I had heard about but until then had not witnessed. There were too many dead men that day. I wanted off the boat. I wanted off the damned boat *right now!* That's all I could think about. Get back to land.

We did return to land, just in time to go out with a patrol for a night in the bush.

I reported to Alpha Company three months after arriving at Cua Viet. As a company corpsman, I went with one of the platoons as it rotated from the battalion area, to the company area, then out to the farthest point for a two-week stint at the platoon base camp at Mai Xi Tai, which was nothing more than the ruins of a Catholic church on the bank of the river. From here we ran patrols both along the river's edge and inland to the free fire zone between the river and the border.

It was during this time of rotations that I drew my turn at tower watch in the battalion area. From this vantage point, I could watch the surrounding countryside with the aid of a Starlight scope. Directly to my front was a large cemetery composed of mounds that marked the graves. On each side of the cemetery were tree lines. Everything could be seen clearly through the scope, bathed in an eerie green glow.

I watched for about two hours as my partner slept on the floor of the tower. Before long I thought the whole world had turned permanently green and was beginning to develop a headache from eyestrain when I saw them. Two figures darted among the mounds of graves, paused and then moved again. I pulled my eyes away, rubbed them and looked again. There they were.

"Hey, wake up!" I said, shaking my partner. "I've got movement out there!"

"What?" he said wearily, rubbing his eyes.

"Get your ass over here and look through this scope. I want to make sure I'm seeing what I think I'm seeing." I moved over and he looked.

"I see them. They're in the northeast corner of the graveyard, about six hundred meters out. I'll call the patrol that's out there and we'll see if we can direct them in."

He picked up the radio and called the patrol. After the preliminary exchange of call signs, he asked, "Are you moving?"

"Negative."

"This ain't no bullshit. If you're moving let me know. We've got two guys moving out there by you."

"We are *not* moving. We're set in the tree line and are *not* moving, over?" said the radio.

"Roger. We'll try to vector you to their position so you can make contact."

As we watched, the Marine patrol could be seen moving slowly in the direction of the two targets. With each direction from the radioman, the patrol adjusted its movement. Finally they were in position, lined up with the two figures in question. What we failed to realize at the time was that we had managed to line the patrol up by placing them beyond the two targets and in line with us. This meant that their point of contact was between them and us.

Then the shit hit the fan. M-16 rounds began striking the tower, pinging off the steel sides and girders as they ended their flight. We hit the deck. There was no way to get out of the tower and there was nothing else we could do.

"Man, that was stupid!" I screamed, finally realizing what we had done. "You're a Marine, I'm a corpsman. You're supposed to know about tactics. That's your job!"

"No shit! I gotta remember: *Never* line 'em up like that again! *Never ever* line 'em up like that again!"

When it was over the tower had taken thirty hits from Marine rifle fire. Two sappers were dead and our way of directing patrols from the tower were forever modified.

I was in Mai Xi Tai when the word came down that there was going to be some activity on the river. Two additional platoons were brought into the area and I watched as two PBR (Patrol Boat River) patrol boats came upriver and passed. They disappeared around a bend and traveled another mile. Arriving at the new location, they went ashore, set up tents and began running patrols out of this area to stem the sapper units that were increasing in their attacks on the boat traffic. We at Mai Xi Tai now became the reactionary force for this element.

Since most patrols were run at night, it came as no surprise when a few nights later, just shortly after midnight, the most God-awful firefight I ever heard broke the stillness. The crescendo of small arms fire was shattering. Long bursts of M-60 fire were joined by the crackle of M-16s. In response, the pop of AK-47s punctuated the American fire. Within minutes the call came. PBRs would pick us up and rush us upriver to join the battle.

I strapped my equipment on, pulled my helmet over my head and picked up my Unit One aid bag, pausing briefly to wonder how many of the supplies inside would be needed tonight. Then we headed for the riverbank. I looked at my watch. It was 0135 hours. It was the first time I was headed into an actual firefight. I was scared shitless.

Mai Xi Tai was on a levee that had been built up from the river. The PBRs pulled into the embankment, their engines purring contentedly in the night as they drifted until the bows came to rest against the bank. I waded out to one and crawled aboard. It would be a quick trip upriver. We were only a few brief minutes from danger.

I thought about the mines as the boats skimmed the dark water. The moon reflected off the surface, casting bright streaks of light across the ripples and illuminating the shadow of the dark bank as the helmsman deftly made slight course corrections. I could tell this was not new to him or his crew. Their faces looked serious—almost worried. So was I.

Then, as we rounded a bend, I could see muzzle flashes emanating from a tree line on the right. From the bank to the tree line was about a hundred yards. The field in between appeared to be a flood plane that flooded when the river swelled with monsoon rains. Short grass offered no cover between the trees and the water's edge. Getting to the embattled Marines was going to be hairy.

My PBR turned right at high speed, listing to starboard as it shifted course. Settling level, the coxswain reduced the throttle and we coasted toward the bank. Too soon the command came to "unass the boat!"

The bow had come to rest against a mud flat that was short of the bank. The crew began yelling, "Get off! Get off *now!*" They wanted back into the safety of the main stream of the river, their mission of depositing us at the objective completed. I crawled over the gunnel and jumped into the chest-deep water. As fast as the sucking mud would allow, I made my way to the bank. I dropped to the narrow beach below the edge of the bank as the PBR motor gunned and the boat backed away for the safety of midstream.

I was the most terrified I had ever been. I was within a hundred yards of an intensive firefight and I knew that we would have to join in to provide as much support as we could. The Marines and the NVA were in the same tree line exchanging fire at close quarters. We would have to figure out who was who and join the Marines. Not always an easy task for a reactionary force. But then, just as we prepared to go over the bank and cross the open field the Marines called on the radio and announced that they had broken contact and pulled back. Then they added, "We've got two full notes and one half note. And we're missing our Doc."

I knew that a "half note" was a wounded man. A "full note" was a KIA. And we all knew who "Doc" was. I began vomiting. I couldn't help it. I puked. I was the only corpsman left and if one was needed now, it was me. I lay there, face in the mud and feet still in the water, and threw up.

The firefight stopped. The patrol called and announced that they were now three hundred yards away from the tree line and the NVA still were there. Then the navy PBR boats came on the radio and said that "Spooky," a converted C-130 gunship, had been called in and was now on station ready to spit death on the stubborn enemy. I rolled to my back to watch the fireworks just in time to see a long string of tracer fire emit from the heavens and arc into the trees like a cutting torch. For almost an hour the airplane circled, shooting its miniguns until nothing could have survived the onslaught. That night I was extremely grateful for the air force. Finally the airplane banked away, its engines droning in the night and fading away as it departed. Within seconds their departure was followed by artillery rounds fired from Cua Viet, each impacting on target in the NVA positions. Finally it lifted.

It was time for us to move in. As we crawled slowly forward through the short grass, the sun started coming up, casting long shadows as it peeked over the eastern horizon. I made the tree line and the first body I found was the corpsman. He had obviously stood up, maybe to help the lieutenant who was lying close by, and had caught a burst in the chest. Next to him was his aid bag. I picked it up thinking that it may be needed. You never could have enough medical supplies—and he wouldn't be needing them anymore. I didn't know what we were going to find but I wanted to be ready.

An RPG (Rocket Propelled Grenade) round had hit a tree. The shrapnel may have hit him and the lieutenant, but I couldn't tell for sure. It was too much of a mess to make a determination. But examining the lieutenant showed that he had also been hit by small arms fire. I moved on.

The patrol that originally made contact rejoined us. Together we swept through the trees. There was no place for the NVA to go, yet as we pressed forward we could see that they were gone. The artillery craters were empty—except for one. In one crater we found an NVA soldier, his head split open from shrapnel, one of the worst wounds I had ever seen. He had been left for dead but was now conscious. I knelt by his side and examined the wound. His scalp had been peeled back, his skull opened and his brain matter exposed. I had never seen a brain exposed like that. It was incredible. I could peer down into his open head and see his brain. I couldn't understand why he was still alive. But he was.

"The ARVNs want to interrogate him," said the platoon commander.

"You can try, but I don't think he'll live long enough," I replied, trying to figure out how to treat him.

"Just bandage him up and let them take it from there."

"This guy needs more than a bandage. He needs surgery," I informed the lieutenant.

"We'll let the ARVNs worry about that."

A helicopter arrived shortly and the NVA and wounded Marine, who had already been treated, were loaded for medevac. Maybe he would make it and maybe he wouldn't. I really didn't care anymore. His friends had killed my friends. The picture of the dead corpsman entered my mind. It could have been me.

I had had enough. I wanted out—away from the reality of war and death. I knew it was only a matter of time, but time was dragging ever so slowly. Finally, after return to the base camp at Mai Xi Tai, my tour in the field ended. I was to be pulled back to Cua Viet to the 3rd Medical Battalion to work in triage at the medevac helicopter landing pad. It was there, as I waited to meet the incoming medevac choppers with their loads of wounded, that the veritable "straw that broke the camel's back" finally broke mine.

We never knew what horrors a medevac flight would bring. I watched with apprehension and fear of what gut-wrenching sights would forever burn themselves into my memory as the helicopter approached. All the radio said was that it was bad. I had seen choppers come in filled with bullet holes, half the crew shot up and the patients lying on the floor in pools of blood. Other flights had come in carrying only body bags, some of which had obviously lain too long in the sun before extraction. All the horrors, all the results of battle, culminated on the medevac pad. It was the receiving point for the refuse of war. I wished I was someplace else as I waited for the chopper to land.

The big Sikorsky H-34 descended toward the pad, but before it could land, the pilot realized that he was facing the wrong direction for the helicopter to be unloaded by the ground personnel. The Sikorsky had only one door on the right side and I was standing on the left. As the machine turned and settled to the ground the door came into view—and with it a glimpse of hell.

Inside were more than twenty burned bodies, each withdrawn in a grotesque pose. Arms and legs stuck up in all directions. Faces were blackened and burned beyond recognition. The smell was overpowering. It smelled like a massive barbecue. As I stared in disbelief men began shouting orders.

"Get them unloaded *stat!* We gotta get that helicopter off the pad. Let's *move!*"

With another corpsman, I carried a stretcher to the gaping door. As I neared a strange thought replaced the horror: *How in the world will we be able to untangle this mess?* They were intertwined like jacks scooped into a pile by some huge child.

"Come on, let's get with the program, people. Get that chopper unloaded!"

I grabbed the wrists of one charred corpse while my partner grabbed its ankles. We lowered him to the stretcher as gently as possible, though *he* would not have known the difference, and began running toward the morgue. As we ran and bounced, one hand from the horribly burnt remains broke off and fell to the ground. The cartilage that held it to the arm had been burned through and the damned hand just *fell off!* I was taken aback. This couldn't be happening. His *hand!* My God, his hand fell *off!* We stopped, laid the stretcher down and I picked up the hand. I gently placed it on the stretcher next to the corpse, as if someone could do something with it later. But I knew, even as I did it, that the effort was ridiculous. For me, the whole scene was just too much.

It was a good thing that I was down to the last couple of weeks. For me, it was time to go home.

14

Hue, 1968

It was in January of 1968 that the war hit its major political turning point. Prior to the Tet offensive, it had appeared that America held the upper hand. But when the NVA and Vietcong attacked 36 of the 44 provincial capitals and five of the six major cities, even waging war in the very heart of Saigon, the generals—and the American public (thanks to biased news reporting)—began to think that the war was a long way from over. Yet, contrary to the propaganda victory the offensive provided the Hanoi government, the operation, tactically, was a disaster. The Vietcong suffered almost 80 percent casualties and after Tet were never again a serious threat. From then on it would be conventional units of the North Vietnamese Army that would carry on the communist cause.

Of the cities that came under fire, the most bitterly contested was the ancient capital of Hue. At 0340 hours on January 31, the 804th Battalion of the 4th NVA Regiment surprised a small contingent of American soldiers in the MACV compound of the New City, the main section of Hue south and east of the ancient walled "Old City" (also known as the "Citadel"). The Americans in the MACV compound fought back valiantly and managed to hold their position. The ARVN Hac Bo (Black Panthers) Ranger Company, trapped in the Old City, were not so fortunate. The combined 800th and 802nd Battalions of the 6th Regiment, reinforced by the VC 12th Sapper Battalion, forced the Rangers back to the ARVN 1st Division Headquarters. This accomplished, the NVA 806th and 810th Battalions took up positions to form a blockade north and south of Hue to seal the fate of those units trapped within.

The American 1st and 5th Marine Regiments were quick to react. Arriving in Hue the same day, they pushed into the city to counterattack the entrenched NVA. But the enemy was determined to stay and fight. The first attempts to rout them failed and the Marines pulled back to regroup and await the light of day.

When the sun rose from the South China Sea the next morning, the Marines attacked the Old City in earnest. This time there would be no pulling back. Three days later they reached the outskirts of the New City.

West of the city, the army's 3rd Brigade, 1st Cavalry Division (Airmobile), supported by its own 1st Battalion, 77th Artillery, blocked the infiltration of three fresh NVA regiments and fought to keep supply lines open for the Marines engaged in close quarters, house-to-house fighting within the city.

After twenty-three days of fighting, the 1st Battalion 5th Marines and elements of the South Vietnamese Army breached the Citadel walls. Three days later, Hue was declared secured. But the victory did not come cheap. Allied casualties numbered 3,228, including 357 ARVN and 142 Marines killed. The NVA lost 4,601 and 45 captured. The civilians lost even more.

Those that could not, or refused, to flee the city in time were caught in a crossfire of Allied and communist artillery, tanks and automatic weapons for the duration of the battle. Others, rounded up by the NVA and Vietcong as government lackeys and corrupt capitalists—mostly government functionaries, teachers, minor civil servants and other educated people sympathetic to the Saigon government—were either executed or buried alive in mass graves outside of the city. After the battle, over 5000 were discovered killed in this manner.

On the outskirts of the city were several villages wherein the inhabitants attempted to continue their daily existence as if the war did not exist. Tending their rice fields, cattle, chickens and pigs came before their own safety. And market day is the most important day of the week. On that day, the village squares would be crowded with farmers and vendors exhibiting their crops and wares along with those that came to buy.

Army Sp5c. Robert Bosma had such a marketplace just across the road from his artillery battery's firing position outside of Hue.

"I expected there to be casualties on both sides," remembered Bosma. "But even though I knew there'd be civilians hurt and even killed in the massive exchanges of gunfire, I expected, being an army medic, to treat wounded *soldiers*— gunners, loaders, ammo humpers, people whose *jobs* put them in positions of danger. Though somewhere in the back of my mind I knew that I might be called upon to handle a civilian casualty, I felt that most would be found by medics in line companies who were farther forward—much closer to the actual fighting or moving through the city—long before I would encounter them.

"There was something about wounded civilians that bothered me—especially in Vietnam where most villagers were either elderly people too old to serve in the military, women, or worse . . . children. The thoughts of torn and bloody civilians, injured or killed simply because they were in the wrong place at the wrong time bothered me. I dreaded such a scenario.

"But I knew, being back in the artillery position, the chances of me having to deal with that were remote.

"I was wrong."

15

Sp5c. Robert E. Bosma
C Battery, 1st Battalion
77th Artillery
1st Cavalry Division
Hue, Tet 1968

During the summer of 1967, Fort Sam Houston, Texas, seemed like a paradise to me. I had left home in Michigan a naive, skinny kid with ears sticking out from my recruit-shaved head looking like a small elephant. Barely twenty years old, I was far from experienced in anything, but I felt like I was ready to solve the problems of the whole world. The medic Advanced Individual Training class that had graduated just before I arrived at the Medical Training Center had about two hundred graduates. Every one of them was now on his way to Vietnam. I had no doubts about the direction my life would take at the hands of Uncle Sam after I completed my brief ten-week preparation as a medic. I, too, would soon be headed into combat.

Classes were normally a droning routine of in-hospital patient care procedures and emergency first aid. But one day in the third week I noted the training schedule listed triage as our four-hour subject to be tackled just after lunch. Classroom activity was pretty boring in the heat of a Texas summer afternoon, especially on a full stomach, and with a mysteriously ominous sounding topic like triage, I was convinced it would be one agonizingly long afternoon.

Our instructor, Staff Sergeant Williams, had just returned from serving a yearlong tour in Vietnam as a medic in the 1st Cavalry Division. As he picked up the controls for the slide projector, I noted the large yellow and black patch on his right sleeve, denoting his time in combat was served with the 1st Cavalry Division. My mind drifted for a moment as I daydreamed about wearing the same bold patch on my own uniform one day.

Sergeant Williams started the slide show. The pictures on the screen were enough to turn the gills of the most profound stoic leaf green. Bodies were scattered in grue-some disarray in a bloody wash of red. Any thoughts of another boring class quickly dissipated.

"Gentlemen, I pray that this is a scene that you never have to encounter," he said, turning to face the class. "Triage is the job of sorting patients in a mass casualty situation to decide who gets treated first."

He paused dramatically, looked directly into our eyes to emphasize the importance of what he was about to say, and then continued. "In this situation, it is your job to decide who will live—*and who will die.*"

The classroom was suddenly so silent that the only sound heard was the drone of the sole window air conditioner. A sense of uneasiness descended upon the class. Students began to squirm in their chairs, and I had a definitely uncomfortable feeling overcome me as I pictured myself running across an open field to patch up a fellow soldier— possibly more than one—wounded in battle. The dreadful realization that I may someday face more than a dozen battered bodies all at once caused chills so profound I felt like I did as a kid on those cold Michigan mornings when I shivered as I walked to school. This was one side of being a medic that I was not quite ready to deal with.

February of 1968 became a month that not only I, but all Americans would forever remember. The Vietnamese Lunar New Year erupted not in revelry and feasting but in a concerted demonstration of will and capability by the North Vietnamese Army and the Vietcong in every province in the country.

Five months after that day in the classroom watching Staff Sergeant Williams point at the grisly slides about triage, I found myself wearing the same patch as he. I had been assigned to C Battery, 1st of the 77th Artillery, 1st Cavalry Division, and had been in Vietnam all of seven weeks. The North Vietnamese Army had just unleashed the violent fury of the Tet offensive across the entire expanse of South Vietnam.

Charlie Battery occupied a tiny strip of land, a point known as PK-17, along Highway 1 six miles north of the ancient Imperial Palace city of Hue. Our six 105mm howitzers were lined up side by side along the south edge of the compound pointing in the direction of the city, and a battered old concrete water tower marked the entrance to our little sanctuary. Our mission was to support the 2/12th Cavalry in their efforts to cut off NVA supply lanes into Hue near the village of Thon La Chu. In the days to come, Charlie Battery would fire over 5000 rounds in this endeavor.

Across the road, east of our battery, was a quaint village of primitive grass and bamboo huts, separated by hardened dirt pathways, that straddled the land between Highway 1 and the lush green banks of the Perfume River. In the center of the village, a framework covered with corrugated tin kept the blistering tropical sun from baking the farm products displayed by the old men and women who sat about chatting, smoking home-rolled cigarettes and chewing betel nut. The intense fighting in the area to wrest control of Hue from the communist forces went on both day and night and involved units from the U.S. Marine Corps, the 101st Airborne Division, and the 1st Cavalry Division. On the afternoon of February 5, I found myself preoccupied with a small pile of artillery shell powder I had enlisted to heat water for C ration hot chocolate when explosions sounded somewhere between our position and the river. Someone shouted "Incoming!" and I dove for cover, assuming 122mm Soviet-made rockets were striking PK-17. Then after only two rounds, there was silence. I wondered what had happened. If it was a barrage, it was a very short one.

Within seconds Charlie Battery's topkick, First Sergeant Loftus, came running to my bunker yelling, "Doc!"

"Get your gear," ordered Loftus after poking his head inside my bunker. "The village across the road took the hits and it's bad. Real bad."

"Okay, Top. Let's go." As I reached for my gear, I felt my stomach knotting up like a sailor's rope, and then a dry lump welling up in my throat the size of a baseball. Each time I heard the cry for "Doc," it was the same. I pulled the strap of my medic's bag over my shoulder, donned my heavy steel pot and nervously ran out of the bunker dreading what Top had described as "bad." I raced past the gun sections and the water tower, across the old highway and into the village. As I ran, I had to use one arm to keep my aid bag from bouncing at my side and the other to hold down my .45 caliber pistol and its holster. Finally arriving at the impact area, I could see that the slides Sergeant Williams had shown back at Fort Sam did little justice to the scene arrayed before me like the back room of a slaughter house.

Both incoming rounds had struck dead center on the village square in an aerial burst. Flesh and limbs torn from the victims were scattered about the little market like so much litter. The sobbing of the survivors squatting alongside the dead was almost as loud as the cries of the wounded. An old woman lay twisted on her back, a ghostly blank stare on her face. Beyond her, a young girl lay crying, her foot sticking out of the skull cavity where the old woman's brain worked busily just moments earlier. An old man screamed *Bac si!* and I saw that his arm had been ripped from its socket and a bubbly red stream of blood and water gushed from a hole in his rib cage. He slipped into permanent silence just as I knelt at his side.

Others were calling for me now, bringing a feeling of helplessness so profound that my shaking began to interfere with my desperate attempts to stop the flood of flowing blood around me. But I had a job to do that no one else could do. I had to triage the casualties, sending those that I thought had a chance of living to a small clearing on the north side of the village to await medevac, while doing what I could to ease the suffering of the others. I forced myself to ignore those I knew had no chance and whose agonizing screams hastened their inescapable deaths. Minutes turned into hours as I fought to keep those frail souls alive.

After the departure of the last helicopter, I walked in a stupor back to Charlie Battery. The hot cocoa I had started to mix that morning would have been a mouth-watering delicacy under other circumstances. That afternoon, it held no appeal at all. Exhausted, dirty and bloody, I crawled into a bunker hollowed into the ground alongside our fire direction center, lay down and cried unashamedly.

Color slides of trauma in a classroom were one thing. The full-color presentation I had just witnessed was entirely something else.

During the twenty-six days Charlie Battery spent on the PK-17 firing position, over 5000 rounds of 105mm ammunition were fired in support of the 2/12th Cavalry as they worked to cut off NVA supply lines into Hue near the village of Thon La Chu.

Prior to the incident in the village, Bosma distinguished himself in action when his unit became heavily engaged with a large enemy force and had suffered several casualties. Incoming hostile fire kept the unit pinned down, but Bosma continually exposed himself to danger as he treated and evacuated the wounded. For this action he was awarded the Army Commendation Medal with "V" for valor.

16

War in the Delta, 1969

Though the combat capabilities of the Americans were second to none, the terrain over the majority of Vietnam favored the communists' hide-and-seek tactics. From the rugged mountains of the north, through the thick jungles of the Central Highlands, and finally the swamps and marshes of the Mekong Delta, locating and destroying the enemy was a tedious and deadly challenge. The Mekong, like the areas to the north, held its own unique brand of warfare.

Covering almost 1500 square miles south and west of Saigon, reaching from the Gulf of Thailand to Cambodia, is the Mekong River delta. Inhabited by an estimated eight million people and constituting the most important rice growing section of Vietnam, it is by far the most important region in the country. And this importance did not escape the communists. Since the early 1960s, the Vietcong had held the upper hand in the Delta until the combined efforts of the army, the navy and the ARVN reduced the enemy's ability to move at will.

Though the Delta mainly consists of a flat alluvial plain and numerous tributaries that make it ideal guerrilla terrain, some roads exist. While the majority of travel was conducted by myriad river craft, with the responsibility for combat operations on the rivers falling to both the navy, with its river patrol boats and troop carriers, and the Army Riverine forces, land operations fell to the infantry and the men who supported them.

Crisscrossed by a complex network of rivers, canals, streams and ditches, the low, poorly drained surface was subject to extensive and prolonged inundation. Monsoon season causes unavoidable flooding as rivers overflow their banks, waterways grow wider and firm ground turns to deep mud. Though the area is suitable for air operations, there was only one hard surface road, Route 4, which extended from Saigon south, through the American army airfield at Can Tho, to Ca Mau, almost to the Delta's tip. Secondary roads were poorly surfaced, if surfaced at all.

Any movement off the roads was limited. And Charlie owned the roads. Nightly forays by the Vietcong left deadly mines and booby traps, often reinforced by ambushes, for any unwary traveler. For the American and ARVN supply convoys that daily traveled the roads between the combat bases, each movement outside the wire was a deadly game. It was the job of the engineers to sweep the roads and clear the mines, an inherently dangerous mission that carried with it its share of casualties.

One of the medics who served with the engineers in the Delta was Sp5c. Stephen Bass. Unlike those who became medics and corpsmen to avoid the war, Bass joined the army to go to war. His motivation was unusual.

"It all started with a book. When I was a kid, I wanted to join the Marines, but one day I read a book about a conscientious objector who had served as an army medic in World War II. He had become a medic so he wouldn't have to carry a weapon, yet could still serve his country. Looked down upon as a CO, he was constantly ridiculed and harassed by the other members of his platoon for being a cowardly noncombatant. Then one day the platoon came under fire and he had to go out and help the wounded guys. Armed only with his medical bag, he made his way under intensive fire to each man. When it was over, he had saved several lives and gained the respect of his men. From then on, he suffered no more harassment. He had proven himself. Even though he was a conscientious objector, he was a brave man who did his duty and helped his buddies. He didn't have to kill people to be a hero. I was impressed by that story and wanted to be like him.

"In July of 1966, I found myself restless and bored. I had dropped out of high school and had just turned eighteen. I had no plans and no job and felt lost in a world that seemed to have no place for me. Still, I knew that somewhere I could contribute something.

"Walking along a downtown sidewalk on a lazy afternoon, I came across a U.S. Army recruiting station. The Vietnam War was going on and the story of the World War II medic flashed into my mind. It was like a revelation. I knew what I had to do.

"Enlisting was no problem—they were taking just about anyone they could—and I had no trouble qualifying to become a medic. But after training at Fort Sam Houston, things began to go wrong. Instead of Vietnam, I received orders for Germany. I tried to have them changed but the army wouldn't cooperate. It was like if you *wanted* to go to Vietnam, you couldn't.

"While in Germany I submitted a new ten-fifty-nine—a request for orders—every month for a year. Every time I picked up a newspaper and saw what was happening in Vietnam and read the casualty figures, I felt my need to be there as a medic grow stronger. Finally, whoever processes these forms that control a soldier's destiny must have tired of seeing my name. One came back stamped 'approved.'

"When I stepped through the door of the air-conditioned plane that had carried me to Vietnam into the blazing sun of Bien Hoa, the heat and smell of the country hit me like a blast furnace in a sewage pit. Squinting through drifting dust and blinding tropical sunshine, I could see sweating GIs bustling around unloading supplies, jets screaming as they took off on missions and trucks, loaded with everything from fresh troops to crates of supplies, belching smoke as they raced off in different directions. There was a sense of urgency in the air. You could feel it.

"Seeing a war movie in an air-conditioned theater or reading a book about combat in the safety of your living room doesn't really prepare you for the reality of war. The oppressive heat or cold, the smells of the battlefield and death, the extreme fatigue of going days on end without sleep, and the discomfort of being trapped in a filthy stinking uniform for a week at a time can't be understood or appreciated until you are actually there. The sights, the sounds and the smells that assailed me seemed like a surrealistic dream, like it wasn't really happening, yet I knew it was and I was there.

"Bien Hoa was only a temporary stop. The replacements on the plane were quickly assigned to other places like they were replacement parts for various machines in a huge factory. I was assigned to the Sixty-ninth Engineer Battalion, Twentieth Engineer Brigade, based at Can Tho Army Airfield in the middle of the Mekong Delta. When I arrived, no one knew me and I felt alone and out of place. The old hands looked at the new guys as both detriments that would require training before being effective and fresh meat for the meat grinder of Vietnam. But for me, that didn't last. Within two days I found that being a medic was different. I was immediately accepted by the troops. When I puzzled over this rapid change of sentiment each time someone found out I was a 'Doc' it was explained like this: 'We gotta take care of you, Doc. If we don't, who's gonna take care of us?'

"It made me feel like I had finally found my niche in life. It made me feel good."

17

Sp5c. Stephen J. Bass
USA, 69th Engineer
Battalion
Can Tho Army Airfield
Mekong Delta, 1969

I had been at Can Tho only three days when Charlie took my combat virginity. I was walking toward the dispensary the morning of my third day in Vietnam when the devil decided to call hell into session. The stillness of the morning was broken with the sound of sirens, starting slowly at first with a low moan that gradually wound up to a high piercing whine that shattered the morning calm. No one had bothered to tell me about the sirens or what they meant. Obviously it was some kind of alert, but for what? I didn't know whether to panic and run toward a bunker or simply wait and see what happened next. What happened next made up my mind.

Incoming! Incoming!

Soldiers ran in every direction as the shouts of warning echoed across the base. Though I still didn't know what was going on—there was no shooting, no explosions of artillery, nothing apparently happening—I decided to join them. As fast as I could, I ran toward the dispensary bunker. Maybe it was only a drill, but if it wasn't I wanted to be where my duty station was and where I could respond if I was needed.

It was no drill. Just as I got to the bunker a string of explosions cracked at the far edge of the camp, resonating across the open with a distant sound that didn't seem too threatening at first, but increased in volume as it moved toward me. Now I knew what all the excitement was about. I dove into the bunker.

I looked around in the dim light. There were about thirty men in the room, and I examined their faces to see if I should be afraid or not. Few seemed very concerned.

"Are we safe here?" I asked the nearest face.

He looked at me questioningly at first, then nodded in recognition of my being a "newby."

"Yeah, these are just mortars. They can't penetrate a bunker. If you're inside, you're safe. It's the rockets that you gotta watch. They don't care if you're in a bunker or not. They'll come through the roof and explode inside. The fuses are different and don't explode on contact."

"Inside?" I asked a bit meekly, studying the ceiling.

"Wipes out a whole friggin' bunker." He stared at me for a moment to let that thought sink in, then gave a slight grin. "But these are only mortars. You only gotta fear *them* if you're caught outside."

As I squinted through the drifting dust shaken from the ceiling by the concussions and listened to the impact of the rounds, I heard something else. Faintly at first, then joined by other, nearer voices, were the cries of men in pain— quickly followed by urgent screams of *"Medic!"* Though we had reached safety, others had not. Men caught in the open before they could reach bunkers had been hit by shrapnel and now lay scattered across the camp like heaps of dirty laundry.

I was scared. I could hear these guys yelling for help, but

sat frozen in fear for what seemed like an hour. Then, like an automatic reaction, my training finally took over. My duty was to the wounded and it sounded like there were plenty out there. In what was in reality only a few seconds I put my instinct for self-preservation aside, dampened my fear as well as I could and started for the door. I almost got trampled.

Since this was the dispensary bunker, the place was full of medics, doctors and litter bearers. As the doctors began preparing to receive the wounded, the medics and litter bearers picked up aid bags and stretchers. I wasn't the first to the door, nor was I the last. Hardly a word had been spoken, but everyone just started doing their job. It was all new to me—it wasn't to them.

"Bass," called one of the other medics as we began to scatter across the camp to find the casualties, "the first thing we gotta do is get these guys in where they'll be safe and can be treated. The doctors can take it from there."

It made sense to me. I began dragging wounded men in as fast as I could. Inside the dispensary bunker, the doctors got busy and began sorting and treating each victim as the severity of the wound demanded. Finally the mortar fire stopped.

We cleaned things up pretty quickly in the vicinity of the bunker and I was just starting to pat myself on the back when I heard my name called.

"Med One . . . Bass, get your team down to the bunker line. They need us down there. They took it pretty good," ordered our dispensary radioman. My rank afforded me the slot of senior aid man, and as such I had three men under me—one assistant aid man and two litter bearers. With these three guys and our ambulance, our medical team was known by the call sign "Med One."

Followed by my team, I dashed toward our "cracker box," a kind of large four-wheel drive ambulance, hit the starter and raced toward the bunker line to see what we could do.

The bunkers and the watchtowers on the perimeter were numbered, and the radio calls coming into the dispensary told us which bunkers to go to. The airfield command bunker's call sign was "Rice Tacker Alpha"—words the

Vietcong would find hard to say should they gain access to one of our radios—and others were "Bravo," "Charlie," and so on. Each time a call for help came in, a "Med Team" was dispatched to the given location. But there were no radios in the ambulances, so once away from the dispensary we were out of contact and could not be updated on the situation. Things would change and we had no way of knowing. For that reason, ambulance duty during an attack was terrifying.

Inside the cracker box were litters and medical supplies, a floor covered with sandbags to offer meager protection against mines, and extra ammunition for the grunts in case they were running low. Instead of a "meat wagon," my cracker box was more like a "war wagon."

There were casualties on the perimeter, but not as bad as the picture I had mentally painted during our quick trip out there. Prior to my orders to Vietnam, I had worked in ICU in a hospital in Germany and had learned quite a lot. Now, the things I learned in ICU really paid off. I felt in control of each situation I encountered and managed to treat or evacuate to the dispensary everyone needing it. By the end of the day we had helped a lot of wounded, sorted out the types of casualties for either local treatment or medevac, and cleaned the area up. Back at the dispensary, with my adrenaline beginning to finally ebb, fatigue began to overwhelm me. I sat down, pulled my helmet off and closed my eyes. It had been a long and traumatic day—a hell of a "welcome to Vietnam."

I soon found out that unlike the medics assigned to hospital duty in the rear who only had certain areas of responsibility, medics assigned to combat units had to do it all. From working in the dispensary to supporting the troops in the field on operations, we were assigned the task. You call, we haul. If something happened to our engineers anywhere in the AO (Area of Operations) and a medic wasn't already on-station, we were sent out—often alone and unescorted. One incident took place that showed me just how dangerous traveling the roads of the Delta could be.

A jeep moved out one day from our fire base and slowly ground its way down the road toward a jungle construction site. Inside, the four occupants scanned the road carefully, as we all did, but failed to see the well-camouflaged antitank mine emplaced to catch the unwary.

In the dispensary, the crackle and static of the radio broke with urgent calls for help. I grabbed the handset, replied to the call and headed for the door.

When we arrived at the scene, a horrible sight greeted us. The jeep was no more. It lay in four pieces, scattered on the road like a collection of scrap metal in a junkyard. The four men who had been inside were in even more pieces. There was nothing anyone could do except pick up and try to identify and bag the pieces with the correct dog tags. I picked up one guy, or what was left of him, by the trunk. There wasn't any head, any arms or legs, only a trunk with the intestines hanging out. I felt sick. I was sent to Vietnam —hell, I *asked* for Vietnam—to save lives, not work for Graves Registration. Then the thought of *how in the hell are they going to identify these pieces and put them in the right boxes when they send them home* entered my mind. The thought that somewhere along the line someone would screw up and mix up the remains bothered me. Though it wouldn't mean anything to the dead, the relatives—what the military called "next of kin"—would be shattered if they discovered that they had buried someone else's son. I mentioned my concern to one of my medics.

"Don't worry about it. Don't mean nothin'. These guys are too messed up for anyone to know the difference. Besides, on cases like this, the casket gets sealed and shipped home with a tag that says Remains—nonviewable, and that's exactly what it means," he explained.

I had seen the shipping containers when I first arrived at Bien Hoa. Oblong metal boxes painted dark green with no markings other than a paper card slid into a small frame at one end. On the card would be a name—last name, first name, middle initial, of course—then a rank followed by a service number and destination. Then the notation Remains—nonviewable.

The shipping containers were lined up on cargo carts that awaited loading on a C-130 parked nearby. It would be a few minutes before they could start their last journey. The plane would have to empty first. Fresh troops filed down the loading ramp and past the boxes on their way to various units—probably to replace those now waiting for space on the plane. Most didn't seem to notice the boxes. Or maybe they just didn't want to.

"Well, let's just do the best we can on getting the right pieces in the same bag." I flushed the thought of what would happen to these guys after we finished. I had enough to worry about with the living without dwelling on thoughts of the dead.

War is not a continuing kaleidoscope of firefights, rocket attacks and ambushes. Soldiers, especially American soldiers, find ways to bring light into the darkness of horror. It was during some of these times when my job crossed the lines that separate the functions of Special Services, the morale officer, and the chaplain. And Christmas is one of those special times of the year when Americans feel homesickness the most. For that, as with most sicknesses, ol' Doc had a cure.

The MPs at the gate waved us right through. After all, who would stop and search an *ambulance* for chrissake? I was carrying sorely needed supplies to the troops—supplies that could very easily mean the difference between life and . . . well, maybe not exactly death, but close.

I slid to a stop in front of one of the bunkers where, by the sounds coming from the lighted interior, it was obvious to the casual observer that a party was going on.

I, along with my assistant, dismounted the cracker box to report on the success of our procurement mission. One crusty sergeant, cracking into a smile, gave orders and two men ran to the rear of the ambulance and threw the doors open. Inside, giggling like schoolgirls sneaking out of class, were six young Oriental ladies of the evening. Procured in town, and strictly off-limits in the base camp, these pretty darlings would not only provide a much needed service to the troops but would fatten their own wallets in the process.

"Merry Christmas, Sarge." I smiled as they led the girls away.

"Merry Christmas, Doc. And thanks."

It felt good to help raise the morale of the troops, and sneaking past the MPs was exciting for my guys—kind of an adventure that broke some of the boredom. But as a medic, I knew that such antics could easily—and often did—come back to haunt me. Though most Vietnamese boom-boom girls insisted on precautions before having sex, not all did. And when they didn't, guys like Sergeant Jackson paid me a visit.

"Doc Bass? I got another of them problems," said the big black soldier that blocked the light of the door with his bulk.

"Let me guess. The 'drip' again?"

"Tha's right, Doc. Okay to see you now?"

"I guess so. Come on in and drop your trousers," I instructed, filling a syringe with ten cc's of penicillin. "You know, Jackson, catching the clap every week is gonna make your pecker fall off."

"But, Doc, I can't help it. It's like a disease. I see some pussy and I just *got* to have some of that shit."

"Then you've just *got* to have some of this shit." I smirked, jabbing his ass with the needle.

Jackson became a regular—there were a few—that visited me almost every week or two. Every time I gave him the same warning and every time he gave me the same reply. It almost was an ongoing joke, but neither of us knew just how close to the truth my warning would eventually prove—but not in the way I expected.

For a medic working in an engineer battalion, there were three basic areas that were dangerous. Within the perimeter of the base camp when the mortars, rockets or sappers attacked; in a remote work-site, surrounded by the jungle and the Vietcong or NVA; or on a convoy or in a single vehicle between these places. Since the size and weight of our equipment dictated that we usually moved by road convoy, and in the Delta there were only a few roads, it didn't take a very brilliant gook to figure out where we would have to travel and plan accordingly. A road ambush is a constant danger and a frightening event. As they say in flying, a convoy—or worse, traveling alone—is hours of tedious apprehension punctuated by seconds of sheer terror.

Our engineers' services were becoming called upon more and more frequently by other units as the war progressed. Each request meant another cross-country trip, and each trip required a medic. But too often, we had to go it alone and answer calls as they came in as best we could with just our little unarmed ambulance.

It was one monsoon night when the clouds opened up like bursting bags of water, marking the ground of the fire base with craters of mud and tiny streams of flowing water when the call came in from Bin Thuy. They had been hit with a mortar and rocket attack. Since these attacks normally stacked up casualties in their fire storm, I was sent along with a couple of grunts to check for wounded. The trip began rather routinely. We bounced, splashed, spun tires and shifted gears as we made our way down the road. Lush green jungle added a peaceful tranquillity to the storybook scene as it passed by. But I knew that the scene was deceptive and the jungle could quickly change from a picture of peacefulness to a scene of disaster. We didn't have to wait long for that to transpire.

The ambush was sprung with a crescendo of automatic weapons fire accompanied by the chatter of small arms. Bullets flew by, and into, our jeep like angry hornets. The driver jammed his foot on the gas pedal and the jeep sprang forward in an attempt to clear the kill zone. He frantically shifted gears, his attention riveted on the road ahead, as we blasted through the ambush. The only way to escape a convoy or vehicle ambush is to drive through as fast as you can. It was learned early in the war that if you stopped, dismounted and tried to return fire, you were dead. It was a kill zone that had been prepared for just such a stupid decision and it meant just what it was called. Screw around in it and you got killed.

We made it through that night, but that wasn't always the case. Within a few days one of our convoys wasn't as fortunate.

It was a scorching day, and just as I began to settle in for a break in the coolness of the dispensary, the inevitable call for medics came over the radio. A convoy had been ambushed and men were bleeding and dying. I saddled up my team and mounted the cracker box.

When we arrived, men were being removed from the vehicles as gently as possible and placed on the ground. I made my way among them evaluating and treating each wound in the order of importance, keeping the four lifesaving steps in mind at all times. I had learned a lot during my time in Vietnam and found that to be the best combat medic you could be, there were four things you thought of and three that you did no matter what: clear the airway, stop the bleeding and treat for shock. To hell with protecting the wound from infection in Vietnam. It couldn't be done. The wound was infected as soon as it occurred. Just patch it up—cover it with a sterile battle dressing—and get them the hell out of there. Let the hospital in the rear treat for infection. I saw more men die from loss of blood, stoppage of the airway, or from shock or fear than anything else. A simple wound could kill a man if he *thought* it would. You had to talk to them, keep them awake and make them realize that they would be all right—even if you were unsure yourself.

The first man had a leg wound. A clean through-and-through gunshot that didn't strike an artery. That was good. A simple pressure bandage would hold that. The second, a shoulder wound that didn't strike anything vital. Again no problem. I moved on down the line. I yelled over my shoulder for a medevac chopper to be called and stopped at the next man. He had been hit with a .30 caliber round through the thigh and was bleeding profusely. He rolled in pain and I tried to calm him. The bullet had broken his femur—the large bone in the thigh—and he was suffering terribly. I gave him a shot of morphine, applied a pressure dressing and splinted it as well as I could. Calming him and explaining to him that he was not serious and would be all right was the main treatment on this one.

As I moved down the convoy, I found more wounded and treated each according to his wounds. I silently thanked God that there were no dreaded sucking chest wounds. I had a fear of chest wounds. They were dangerous sonsofbitches.

Guys died from them. There was little you could do to handle them. Sometimes a man would make it and sometimes he didn't no matter what you did. I hated that type of trauma. But that day I did not encounter any casualties I could not handle. Finally I reached the end of the column and heard the medevac choppers approaching in the distance. My heart was racing, my adrenaline surging. Now it was simply a matter of loading up the casualties and turning them over to the doctors in the rear. My charges would make it and I felt a great sense of satisfaction. Little did anyone know that I had a tendency to panic if someone was dying and I couldn't do anything about it. I felt a great sense of responsibility to my patients. I was there to help them—to save them if I could—and I didn't want anything to go wrong. I wanted to be in control, but I knew that sometimes that would not happen. I dreaded that. I couldn't face the prospect of making a mistake or doing something that caused the death of one of *my* charges. When they were healthy they were the commander's men. When they were wounded, they were mine. I watched with relief as the last Huey banked away in a cloud of dust and disappeared into the distance.

I had made it through another day in Vietnam. I was even beginning to mark my short-timer's calendar. Just a few months left. So far, so good.

We drove back to Can Tho, and just as I climbed out of the cracker box, I noticed two litter bearers loading a casualty up for transportation to the airfield. I walked over to see if it was anyone I knew.

"Jackson!"

"Hi, Doc. Looks like I'm getting out of here."

"What happened?" I asked the big black sergeant.

"Caught some shrapnel, Doc. You were wrong. I made it all the way through Vietnam and my pecker *didn't* fall off." He grinned.

"Well, you're damned lucky it didn't," said one of the litter bearers. "Take a look," he said to me, motioning at Jackson with his head.

I pulled back the blanket and saw a mass of bandages— covering his *crotch*. I looked up questioningly.

"Got one of his nuts blown off."

"But I still got another one—and my pecker!" Jackson grinned again, pointing proudly at the bandages.

"One inch higher," I said, mockingly, holding my thumb and forefinger slightly apart for him to see, "just *one* inch higher, and you'd be a *girl!*"

Sometimes being a medic in Vietnam had its humorous moments. Sometimes. But very damned seldom.

18

No Friendly Bunkers

The Nixon administration took office promising a different policy for the war in Vietnam. Part of Nixon's plan was a concept of "Vietnamization" wherein the Vietnamese forces would take over combat operations from the Americans, culminating with the eventual withdrawal of American combat forces altogether. For this to happen, several things had to occur. First, the ARVN would have to be modernized with the latest equipment. This could be done as the American units pulled out and gave their tanks, helicopters, APCs and weapons to the South Vietnamese. But the timing was crucial. The ARVN would have to be of sufficient morale, fighting capability, numbers and level of training to stand on their own in the areas they inherited from the Americans as they withdrew. The tactical timing was also crucial. The North would have to sue for a peaceful cease-fire and subsequently withdraw the North Vietnamese troops, and guarantee respect of the 1954 Demarcation Line, now called the demilitarized zone, that ran roughly along the 17th Parallel. Without the powerful military presence of the American forces, the ARVN would stand little chance against the combined strength of the NLF and the NVA. It was essential that they withdraw.

But for this to happen, Hanoi, after its unexpected political victory during Tet—even though it suffered grievous casualties and was soundly defeated tactically—would have to be made to not only listen but to agree. It was now America's turn to go once again on the offensive.

Operation Rice Farmer, a joint U.S./ARVN effort, kicked off 1969 consecutively with a massive all-ARVN operation in southern IV Corps code-named *Quyet Thang*. This would last all year and claim 88,000 enemy dead. In the north, along the DMZ and around Phu Bai and Da Nang, the Marines and ARVN conducted deep penetration operations all the way to the Laotian border in search of the elusive enemy.

But the NVA and VC fought back. In January and again in February, massive rocket attacks struck 110 targets in South Vietnam including Saigon and Da Nang. For their sins, communist units were sought out and destroyed in a renewed fury. Southwest of Da Nang, the 7th Marines pursued their nemesis' 141st and 31st NVA Regiments on Operation *Oklahoma Hills*. Farther to the south, U.S. and South Vietnamese troops moved into Cambodia to destroy communist sanctuaries in the "Parrot's Beak," while massive B-52 strikes mounted against the supply lines on the Ho Chi Minh Trail. Though the intensity of the fighting did not reach the level of that in 1968, the year would prove that Nixon's intentions would not fall into place as quickly as the White House expected. The enemy was still not beaten and showed no signs of giving up.

Though the combat capabilities of the Americans were second to none, the terrain over the majority of Vietnam favored the communists' hide-and-seek tactics. From the rugged mountains of the north, through the thick jungles of the Central Highlands, and finally the swamps and marshes of the Mekong Delta, locating and destroying the enemy was a tedious and deadly challenge. But sometimes the enemy came to you.

And when he did, it was only after very careful planning and intricate preparation. Spies infiltrated American and

South Vietnamese bases and installations disguised as civilians or ARVN soldiers to study the layout. They paced off distances between such things as crew-served weapons pits, communications and headquarters bunkers, and even dispensaries and hospitals. This information was then incorporated into an attack plan. Maps were made—often of silk cloth to counter moisture—and detailed sand table mockups of the camp were built to brief the attack force. Every detail was studied until the entire installation had been memorized by the soldiers. The assault force was then broken down into teams, with each assigned a specific target or group of targets. Some would support the attack from outside the installation's defenses while others would penetrate to wreak havoc from within.

From a camp's perspective, the attack would begin—usually well after dark—with a barrage of rocket, artillery or mortar fire. This created confusion, pinned down the defenders (often away from their assigned defensive positions) and caused the first casualties. Next would come automatic weapons and rifle fire from one or more sides of the perimeter. This crisscrossing waist-high fire continued to keep the defenders pinned down and added to the casualty list.

Then the wire would be hit. *Sapper* (an early British Army term for engineer) teams would by then be in position to breach the defensive strands of barbed concertina and apron-string wire, having earlier cleared paths through the mine fields to reach their breaching points. They might cut the strands to open a larger gate, or simply lie down upon it to allow others to jump over. If the wire was stacked, as in the case of "triple-strand" concertina (two coiled rows on the bottom forming a base for the top row), they would carefully part the coils and, stripped almost naked to keep from snagging the barbs, slither through.

Once the assault and demolition teams were inside, the support element's fire either shifted or ceased altogether to permit the infiltrators to sprint across the camp toward their objectives. Fighting positions and bunkers would be hit, and if possible, occupied by the assault teams as the demolition teams—sometimes only individuals carrying backpacks full of explosives—raced toward their assigned targets.

Satchel charges or grenades would be thrown through firing ports, or worse, sappers with explosives strapped to their bodies would dart through bunker doorways to detonate their deadly cargo inside. In this way the larger command bunkers and communications centers would be eliminated. The camp, now divided up into pockets of resistance with no unifying command element, became chaotic segregated firefights.

In the confusion, bunkers and fighting positions changed hands—often several times. What was once a friendly position could within minutes become an enemy-infested strong point. For the corpsmen and medics, this was a terrifying dilemma.

"What I feared most was the fact that things changed," said Steve Bass, reflecting on his base camp ambulance duty. "If the VC got inside the camp we never knew exactly who was in control of a bunker or position. A bunker that called for help one minute might be full of bad guys by the time we got there, and we had no way of knowing until we started taking fire. It was bad enough just trying to get there in that big boxy ambulance with the huge target painted on the side. It was worse when we arrived only to find that the bunker had changed hands."

In the early morning hours of January 13, 1969, Steve Bass would come to realize his worst fears.

19

Sp5c. Stephen J. Bass
Can Tho

January of 1969 found Can Tho in a relaxed mood. All was quiet around the camp and I was getting short. I had been out on several operations and did basically what every other combat medic had done, and I was feeling pretty good about my tour. Most of it was behind me and surely I could handle about anything I would encounter in the final weeks before rotation back to "The World." The nightly mortar attacks had dribbled to a halt about forty-five days before and things were getting lax inside the base camp. I began to feel that my stay in Vietnam was ending in a rather anticlimactic way and found myself getting about as slack as the troops on the perimeter. You could see it everywhere. Guys were getting overconfident and lazy. They could be seen playing volleyball and having cookouts. A general feeling of security pervaded the camp. Maybe the war was winding down and we hadn't been told, but we could feel it. This should have been a warning sign, someone should have noticed, but no one did. If the grunts weren't worried, why should I be?

It was my night to stand CQ (Charge of Quarters) in the dispensary. The CQ had the job of listening to the radio in case a medic or ambulance was needed, and I sat in a chair listening to the static on the radio when fatigue began to come over me. I had been up for too many hours and was on the edge of exhaustion. Maybe I could sit back and grab a little nap. The radio was quiet and it seemed safe to grab a few minutes of shut-eye. There hadn't even been a radio check from the command bunker in over an hour. I leaned back in my chair and within seconds fell fast asleep.

In what seemed like only a few minutes I was jerked awake by a horrendous explosion. The entire bunker shook. Dust drifted down from the ceiling and the lights flickered. I looked around frantically and glanced at my watch. I had been asleep for almost two hours. Was this an attack? How long had it been going on? Had anyone tried to call me on the radio? I was on the verge of panic. I would surely be court-martialed! Almost ready to go home and I was going to end up in Leavenworth!

The radio was dead silent. I turned the volume up and listened intently. Perhaps it was nothing, or whatever it was was just beginning. Immediately the radio came alive, and frantic calls for help began to fill the static. Other people who were sleeping in the dispensary had by now awakened and began running past me toward the door to the dispensary bunker screaming, "Incoming . . . incoming!"

Incoming? If it was, it damned sure wasn't just mortars. Whatever was hitting us outside was big—damned big.

I couldn't leave because I was on call. I had to stay with the radio in case a medic team was needed. More rounds began to fall, each seeming to land closer to the dispensary. The ground shook and fear began to build in gut-wrenching waves as I hunkered by the radio table. Must be artillery. Then I heard the telltale sound that proved me wrong. Instead of the familiar whistle, it was a nerve-shattering *screech!*—the sound of rockets!

Explosion followed explosion. Even those in the bunkers wouldn't be safe. Ambulance teams began reporting in to the dispensary and I sent them out on the calls as they came in. Finally, all the teams but mine were out, and I no longer had contact with any of them. Then it happened.

"Med Charlie Poppa, this is Bunker Two-Three, we need medics. We're under attack . . . they're everywhere!" I picked up the mike and tried to get a better report of the situation but the terrified young voice on the other end could only repeat his frantic calls for help. Bunker Two-Three was a command bunker near the wire—one with a lot of people inside.

"Okay, guys, it's our turn. Let's get out there," I ordered as I grabbed my helmet and headed for the door.

Outside, I could hear for the first time, joining the explosions of the mortars and rockets, the crackling sounds of small arms fire and the staccato bursts of automatic weapons, both ours and the VC's. Red and green tracers crisscrossed overhead and along the perimeter, and men could be seen darting for cover under the illumination of parachute flares floating overhead, casting eerie shadows across the ground.

Down on the perimeter, a jeep with a large searchlight slid to a stop behind the bunker line and lit up the night sky, searching across the distant tree line. To one side a machine gun opened up, sending brilliant red tracers streaming into the trees. To the other side rapid bursts from M-16s sparkled in the dark. The camp seemed in a state of psychedelic mass confusion.

As the light played across the open field on the far side of the wire I could see several figures darting about wearing black pajamas. They were close and getting closer. Several went down, but more replaced them and they continued to advance toward the wire.

We raced toward Bunker Two-Three, bouncing over shell craters and ruts. But in the time between the first call for help and our arrival, as had so often happened in the past, things had changed.

"There's a bunch of new guys on the perimeter," yelled one of my medics. "They'll be shooting at anything and everything."

"I know. Watch your asses and take it low. Be sure to

identify yourselves before you approach any position. I don't want anyone hurt by 'friendly fire,'" I cautioned.

I stopped short of the bunker and we quickly threw the ambulance doors open and began unloading litters and our large aid bag. With my medics and litter bearers following me, I ran toward the emplacement.

It was pitch-dark and hell was erupting around us as we ran toward the bunker. Nearby, panic had set in among the new troops and some positions were firing at each other while others were shooting at anything that moved. I took this into consideration and used caution as I approached. As expected, we began to take fire from the bunker and immediately dropped to the ground and identified ourselves.

I could hear calls for help from within the bunker, followed by single gunshots. After a few of these gunshots, the screams for help ceased. I got to my feet and started forward again, followed by my team.

Automatic weapons fire from the bunker again laced the air. I couldn't believe it. I screamed in frustration at the bunker.

"Hey, fuckheads, it's us . . . medics! Cease fire, goddamnit!"

But they didn't cease fire. It intensified, kicking up spurts of dust around us.

"Stupid sonsofbitches!" I screamed at the bunker. Then, to my people, "Get back to the cracker box and take cover. These fuckers don't know what in the hell is going on." We made our way back to the ambulance and hunkered behind it.

A grunt from one of the infantry field units slid to the ground beside me. "Goddamn, Doc, that bunker's been taken by the VC. It's full of gooks!"

"No shit?" I asked, realization coming over me for the first time. "No *wonder* they tried to kill us! Listen," I said, drawing the sergeant near, "we've got wounded in there. We've got to get to them and try and see what we can do," I pleaded.

"Okay, Doc, we'll do our best." The squad leader grinned.

Craig Roberts

He disappeared into the dark at a crouch, his troops following. I grabbed my aid bag and hurried after him.

As we neared the bunker, muzzle blasts from AK-47s again split the night. But this time, M-16 fire from experienced field troops that knew what they were doing replied in turn.

We maneuvered closer and closer in short rushes, each time being covered by a fire team that had gained ground. Soon we were at the door of the bunker and the first infantryman darted inside—followed by a second and then a third. I followed. It was dark inside and I could see the darkness sporadically replaced by the strobe light effect of muzzle blasts. Within minutes all was quiet.

We lighted flashlights and began searching the bunker. I was horrified at what I saw. Sixteen Americans lay dead—most still in their bunks. They had been killed as they slept by eight sappers who had crept inside before the mortar attack. Thoughts of sleeping on radio watch raced through my head. What if the sappers had picked the dispensary instead of this bunker? Not only me, but all the other medics and doctors who slept there would now be dead. I felt faint.

A young PFC lay slumped over the radio table. He must have been the one I spoke with when he called frantically for help. He had died at his post. I looked at the Vietcong. Some didn't look over fifteen or sixteen years old. A few had B-40 rocket grenades and explosive charges strapped to their bodies that could be detonated by the bearer at will. They had been killed before they could do so. Chills ran through me. What if one had remained alive until we had all entered the bunker and then blown himself—and us—to hell?

For forty-five days the Vietcong had left Can Tho in peace. Then, when we least expected it, they came back with a fury. I had been deceived into thinking that we must be winning the war and that it was in the process of winding down. I was wrong.

For his actions on the night of January 13, 1969 when the VC overran Can Tho, Sp5c. Stephen Bass received the Bronze Star with "V" device for valor.

20

War in the Mountains

Though the men of the 3rd Marine Division faced elements of six North Vietnamese regiments along the demilitarized zone, contacts in the first days of 1969 had been light. But each day brought more intelligence that something was brewing across the border. Then, after an extensive effort to gather intelligence proved successful, it was determined at the end of January that enemy strength had increased to almost 37,000 personnel within the Zone and Quang Tri Province, the northernmost province of South Vietnam that bordered the DMZ. To the west, in the A Shau Valley and across the border in Laos, signs of increasing enemy traffic became apparent. Roadwork was being carried out on Route 548 in the valley and on Route 922 in Laos. Everything pointed toward an attempt to recreate Tet of 1968.

The Marine combat bases were not living up to the Marines' expectations. They were too large and unwieldy and had become a system of static defenses, cutting down on the mobility of field troops in favor of denying the enemy terrain by use of artillery. Maj. Gen. Raymond G. Davis, a

World War II Medal of Honor winner, had taken command of the division the previous May and quickly analyzed the situation. He felt that the only way to find, fix and kill the enemy was to leave the combat bases and go after him in the rugged jungles and mountains that gave him refuge.

Under new tactical guidelines, 3rd Division Marines advanced rapidly into proposed areas of operations to establish forward artillery positions defended by a minimum of infantry personnel. They occupied key terrain features on high ground that commanded the surrounding terrain. Each base was mutually supporting to discourage enemy attempts at cutting-off and surrounding an individual base. Each was within eight kilometers of the next and each had the ability to shoot 3000 meters beyond its neighbor to discourage enemy mortars and infantry attacks.

Once inserted into these locations, Marine rifle companies and even entire battalions, could move rapidly throughout the area to be searched. This technique created a "Denial Area" up to three kilometers deep that stretched west from Con Thien, across Mutter's Ridge just south of the DMZ, to within six kilometers of the Rockpile on the west.

Bordering the Denial Area east of Con Thien, across to Gio Linh, south to Dong Ha and back west to Cam Lo, was a strangely flat piece of terrain dubbed "Leatherneck Square."

In these areas and the thickly jungled mountains to the southwest, the grunts would be faced with more than the enemy. Heat, disease, tropical ulcers and jungle rot would pose as great a threat as the Vietcong and NVA. In camp—when not being struck by the big guns from the north—it would be the sanitation problems that kept the "Docs" busy. From microbes you couldn't see that caused gut-wrenching dysentary to rats as big as opossums that spread disease and would eat or bite anything, the corpsmen confronted daily challenges in their efforts to take care of the men who took care of them.

Hospitalman Tim Roth, a former private-care male nurse from the San Fernando Valley, never suspected what fate had in store for him when he enlisted in the navy to avoid serving in combat.

"When my letter from Uncle Sam arrived inviting me to report to the army, I knew I had to immediately do something or I would end up in Vietnam. I didn't want to end up like my next-door neighbor and two of my high school buddies who had already gone over. They were all dead. Nor did I want to come home like some of my other friends who suffered horrible wounds and disabilities. With my medical training and background experience, I knew that I could be of service in some nice safe rear area job—maybe working with the wounded when they came back. I didn't mind that.

"I rushed down to the navy recruiter, a congenial fellow who did not hesitate to paint a very rosy picture of the navy. The bottom lines were: Yes, I could stay in medicine. Yes, I could receive further training in this field, and yes, it would be easy for me to go on to become a navy doctor with the navy footing part of the bill. It sounded great.

"He never once mentioned the Marines.

"I *did* get my medical training. But as soon as I completed it, I also got the Marines—in Vietnam. And in 1969 that meant the DMZ. For someone who wanted to work in the rear, I was being sent as far 'forward' as you could get."

21

HN Timothy P. Roth
Mike Company
3rd Battalion
3rd Marine Regiment
Quang Tri Province, 1969

Con Thien. It was something like a scene out of a World War I movie, or maybe on the surface of the moon. It had been bombed flat; cratered and shell-holed until there was little left except stumps, rocks and holes in the ground. Just looking at it made you realize it was a bad place—an *evil* place. A place where death haunted the grounds like a stray dog. Too many good men had died there, and too many more would follow. Con Thien was Mike Company's home, which meant it was now my home as well, and the area around us our stomping grounds.

My feeble attempt to avoid the infantry when I received my draft notice had been of no avail. Here I was, with the grunts, in the most horrible place I'd ever seen in my life. It was like a nightmare come true.

Whenever Mike Company drew a mission, whether it was to look for the "hard hats" (the nickname we gave the NVA because of their distinctive brimmed sun helmets), do a recon, retrieve a body, or join a sweep, the threat of a rain of artillery and mortar fire hung over us like an ominous fist. The NVA were close, within spitting distance. And *that's* when they were across the border, only three klicks away. But most of the time, they came south and did their best to mess with us in our own backyard.

The DMZ was only respected by the Americans. The NVA couldn't care less about it. It was a safe haven where they massed their troops, ready to strike whenever they felt like it—and they felt like it a lot. To keep them at their distance and off balance, and to kill them at every chance, we drew patrols and search operations so often it seemed like we never slept.

And neither did Recon. Those guys went places even Superman feared to tread. Sometimes it got them into trouble.

The word came. A Recon unit had gotten itself surrounded and was taking heavy fire. Mike Company was called to go out and find them and get them out if possible. I grabbed my medical gear and joined the others as we mounted tanks for a piggyback ride across the disheveled countryside. Once everyone had scrambled aboard the steel monsters, it was "Mad Mike to the rescue."

About two hours out we entered high pampas grass. I was riding over the left track, just in front of the turret, on the second tank assigned to my squad. As we rocked along, jerking, and clanking and throwing dust into the air, I began enjoying the ride. It sure beat walking. It was unusually peaceful and I relaxed to take in the sights.

Suddenly there was a tremendous explosion, immediately followed by the smell of burnt gunpowder and a violent shock. I was propelled about thirty feet through the air, tumbling head over heals, to land flat on my back, the wind knocked out of me. My tank had hit a mine.

Gasping for breath, my vision slowly clearing, I looked up

to see the face of Staff Sgt. Roy Hoatland, a rugged NCO known as "The Old Man" because he was older than all the lieutenants—and even the Skipper. His face split into a grin when he realized I was not injured, then he began to laugh.

"What are you laughing at?" I demanded as I picked myself up from the ground, regaining my breath.

"Quite a show, Doc."

I looked around. Four other Marines had been blown off the tank and all were regaining their feet unharmed. Thank God for that.

"Seems you guys got the mine that we missed," Roy said. "My tank rolled right over it and it didn't go off. Must have been an old French mine. The NVA jobs usually don't fail. Welcome to Vietnam, Doc."

I dusted myself off and went back to the tank to discover that a member of the tank crew had not been as fortunate as those who had ridden outside. The tank gunner had a broken neck from being slammed into the closed hatch. I supervised his removal, being careful to not move him any more than necessary, then got him ready for medevac.

After the chopper left, I shouldered my pack and rejoined Hoatland. "Pretty bad, eh, Roy?"

"Just another day in Vietnam, Doc," he replied, matter-of-factly. I was amazed at his callousness, but then he had seen a lot more than I had. For me, this was only the beginning. It was my first experience treating a wounded man in combat. And the most bizarre thought was that my first casualty had been caused by the French—fifteen years after Dien Bien Phu.

Before I could get used to working in the area along the "Z," we got called south. Da Nang had had some trouble. The NVA and VC had made quite a nuisance of themselves, working out of what intelligence labeled "Base Area 112," an area west of Da Nang along the Laotian border. Along with the 1st and 5th Marines, in a major operation called Taylor Common, the 3rd was temporarily pulled out of Con Thien to help penetrate the area, to occupy hilltops and set up fire bases to cover the Laotian border. Our specific task was to secure Objective Mace, Hill 375.

Before we were to arrive, the air force, flying C-130

transports, was to drop 10,000-pound bombs—only one of which could be carried in each airplane—on the narrow ridge lines in an attempt to clear them of jungle for us. But for some reason these horrendous bombs failed to remove the thick secondary growth of canopy that covered the terrain in Base Area 112. The jungle—and the enemy—were still thick and still there.

I had never worked in a canopied area before. It was a totally foreign type of warfare. The density of the jungle could hide a man only a few feet away. The vines and scrub pulled at your legs at every step and exhausted you so quickly that you didn't think you could move another foot. I had never seen anything like it. It was terrible.

We moved through this rugged terrain for over two sweat-drenching weeks. I was faced with treating everything from heat stroke to the worst cases of jungle rot I had ever seen. Huge leeches fell on us and had to be removed. The water was not fit to drink and for those who tried, dysentery consumed their already weakened frames so rapidly that they immediately began to lose massive amounts of weight. I felt that the best weapon we had against the NVA was BA 112. Let *them* have it. Make *them* live here.

It was during these backbreaking days of Taylor Common that I developed an affinity with the Marines. I found out how much I needed them, and they found out how important "Doc" was on day-to-day operations—even if we hadn't taken fire.

"Doc, take a look at my back."

It was our radioman. I waited for him to remove the heavy PRC-25 radio from his back then lifted his shirt anticipating the worst. I had by now had my share of experience with jungle rot, but didn't really have any way to treat it. Nothing in the military supply system seemed to faze it. I wanted to declare war against it; to attack it and win, but I didn't have the ammunition. It became a personal thing—a vendetta.

"My God! Your back looks like a pizza!" I exclaimed, examining his sores. His entire back consisted of seeping craters caused by the fungus. Any scratch, any pimple, any nick, turned into great gaping craters that seeped pus and rotted. It was horrible.

"Can you do anything, Doc?"

"I'll do what I can, but try and get someone else to hump the radio for a while." I dabbed his skin with what I had but knew it would do little good. I swore that I would find a solution . . . someday.

When Taylor Common finally ended, it was stamped a complete success. The 3rd Marines alone chalked up 132 NVA killed and 850 captured. We discovered and captured thousands of pounds of clothing and rice, great amounts of documents and hundreds of mortar and artillery rounds. It indeed was a "base area."

But the jungle rot had kicked our butts.

After returning to Con Thien I took inventory of my medical supplies. There was nothing there that would fight the "rot." I tried ordering everything that the military could send that might help, but nothing that arrived worked. Everything they sent was garbage. That's when I decided to escalate my war.

I wrote my parents, explained the problem and asked for some help. I wrote all the major drug companies and did the same. I requested anything that they wanted tested in Vietnam and said that I needed all the samples they could send. I pleaded. I begged. I mailed the letters, then sat back to wait.

Time passed and I had almost given up hope when one day a chopper circled overhead, dipped its nose and descended for a landing. Aboard was our daily mail delivery, and for me, something special.

Looking nothing like angels bringing an answer to my prayers, two leather-skinned Marines struggled under the weight of a mailbag from the chopper as they made their way toward me. Could it be?

"Hey, Doc. I don't know what this is, but it's damned heavy. Looks like you got a 'Care' package."

Inside the mailbag was a huge box that appeared as if it had been left overnight in a tiger's cage. It was battered, beaten and crushed, but it still held its contents intact. I tore it open.

Inside, much to my joy, was the greatest supply of various salves, creams and ointments I had ever seen. Several of the drug companies had come through, sending their supplies to my parents who in turn sent them to me in one box. In spite of the military supply system, I had managed to get what I needed for my personal war. Now I had the ammunition. I even had more than I needed, so I shared it with the corpsmen in the other companies.

Within days, the jungle rot problem in Mike Company had receded. It didn't completely leave—it never would—but I damned sure had it on the run.

Jungle rot was bad stuff. So were the various types of traumatic wounds suffered from gunshots and shrapnel. But one particular type of wound was by far the most difficult to deal with, and for me, the most horrible to behold. I first encountered it on a company operation in the jungle along the Laotian border.

As we snaked our way through the bush, moving slowly and as quietly as possible in the ink-dark night, ghostly silhouettes outlined beneath the occasional parachute flares were the only thing I could see that reassured me that I was not alone. A few more hours and it would be daylight. I would feel much better then. At least we could *see* any signs of the enemy. But before dawn could light our way, it happened.

A brilliant light and muffled *pop!* sent clusters of miniature stars arcing into the air trailing fingers of white smoke. I knew immediately what it was. White phosphorous. Oh my God!

Corpsman! Doc! After seeing the flash I knew the inevitable call would come. I raced forward as fast as the tangling vines and undergrowth would permit. Ahead, one of the Marines had been within the burst radius of the explosion, whatever it was. It could have been a booby trap, a mortar round, or even a WP grenade. It didn't matter and I didn't care. I had a man down and that's all that counted.

When I got to him, he was on the ground, passed out. But his back still flamed as the particles burned their way deeper into his body. I was taken aback at the sight and was at a loss. The Marines gathered to watch ol' Doc take care of their wounded buddy, but what could I do? I couldn't put my hands on it, I couldn't bandage it, I felt helpless as the phosphorous continued to do its deadly work. The smell of burning flesh assailed my nostrils as the white burning metal, almost with a life of its own, burned deeper into his flesh.

I knew I had to cut off the supply of oxygen to the chemical to put it out. The only way to do that in the bush is to pack the wound with mud. I had to find some quickly.

Below us, at the base of a ravine, was a stream. I picked up the unconscious form and threw him down the side of the hill, following as fast as I could slide and tumble after him. At the bottom, I dragged him into the water.

Even underwater, the damned stuff kept burning. But it was there I could fill my hands with mud. I scooped handfuls of it out of the streambed and stuffed it into the gaping holes, which by now were already cauterized from the heat of the WP (White Phosphorous). Once the oxygen supply had been stemmed, the burning stopped. The mud would have to remain until he reached the rear where it could be removed in a controlled environment. If the mud dried and broke away, the particles would reignite and the process would start over.

Finally the medevac chopper arrived and we loaded him up. As it pulled away, I had my doubts as to whether he would make it. I hoped so. But at least I had succeeded in reacting properly in as little time as possible. It was my first experience with a WP casualty, and I felt that I had done as much as I could. With each new casualty, with each new experience, I tried to distance myself from my emotions and do the job as professionally as I could. But corpsmen are only human—and so are our emotions. I continued to do my job whenever I was needed, but now it became a process of fighting back the feelings . . . and fear of failure. I would never lose the compassion.

After the steaming jungles and rugged mountains, Con Thien seemed like a welcome respite from hell. As bad as it was, at least we could get a hot shower, some new uniforms, receive mail and maybe even see a movie. Con Thien also began to seem more like home as now we realized how much it meant to live in the safety of bunkers. We still had to run patrols out of the camp and had to stand watches on the bunker line, but it wasn't anything like humping the mountains and living in the jungle of BA 112 with nothing more than a poncho liner to curl up in.

Yet, Con Thien, with all these "amenities" still held an enemy within. As with any combat base, the refuse of war quickly built up faster than it could be disposed of. Trash dumps containing everything from expended artillery round casings to semiempty C ration cans bred rats—rats that grew as big as 'possums. Great fat rodents that held no fear of America's finest fighting force. They were the kings of infiltration and would, like the NVA, appear when and where they wanted.

To combat this enemy within, we prepared elaborate devices and plans. Most failed. It soon became a duel between man and beast. And with the Marines' penchant for solving problems with firepower, weapons began to appear in modified form.

"What are you going to do with that?" I asked the radioman who shared my bunker.

"Gonna do some rat killin'," he replied, jamming a clip into his .45 pistol.

"With a forty-five? Hey, man, that thing will stop a water buffalo."

"I changed the load. Took the bullets out of a few shells and packed 'em with wax from the artillery containers. I'm keeping a separate clip loaded with 'rat loads' for when the buggers decide to visit us."

I watched as he laid the pistol on a shelf and hung up a flattened piece of C ration case on the wall.

"What's that?"

"Scoreboard."

A few nights later, I came in off watch tired and hungry. I sat wearily on my sleeping shelf—we didn't have cots or bunks—and prepared my favorite C rations meal: crackers and peanut butter. A few minutes later, having eaten all I could stand, I lay back, with the half-empty can still resting on my chest, and went to sleep. My sleep didn't last long.

Pop!

143

I jerked awake at the sound. A shot had been fired in my bunker. The thought of sappers flashed through my head: *They're in the bunker!* But instead of sappers, I saw the radioman standing in the doorway, a smoking forty-five in his hand.

"You owe me one, Doc," he said, crossing to his scoreboard and making a mark. I looked around to see what he had done. There, on my chest, was a huge ugly rat, its eyes staring lifelessly at me, his quivering claws covered with peanut butter and cracker crumbs. I smacked it away with a backhand.

"Yeah, I owe you one. *Yechh!*"

The longer I was in Vietnam, the more I became hardened. By summer, I was a lean, mean, fighting machine. I was a bad-assed corpsman in a bad-assed unit—until the early morning hours of June 17, 1969, in Leatherneck Square. That day, the John Wayne world as I knew it, came to an end.

We were on line, walking through flatlands covered with pampas grass, when the first shot rang out. To my right, on the flank, a Marine named Bill "Stoney" Stone went down. Then before we could react, more shots followed. AK-47 shots. It was an ambush—a big one.

"Come on, Doc. Let's go!" cried Roy Hoatland. I got to my knees and followed him and the radioman to Stoney, avoiding incoming fire as well as we could. Finally, after successfully crossing the kill zone, we slid to the ground by his side. I ripped open my aid bag as Roy turned him over. It was too late. He had taken a round between his eyes, leaving half of his head still in the helmet that lay nearby.

Before I could react to this horrible sight, more bullets buzzed overhead, cracking as they passed my ears. By the sound of the fire, we were obviously outnumbered. A battalion of NVA had sprung an elaborate U-shaped ambush, and in the confusion, as Marines tried to react and take up firing positions to counter the onslaught, more men screamed and went down. I crawled forward. As I did so, I could hear calls for corpsman in every direction. The three other corpsmen in the company, each in his own pocket of dead and dying, crawled from man to man, applying battle dressings, IVs and tourniquets.

In front of me were three wounded Marines. One had a head wound—he was dead. The other two had belly wounds. I knew that I had to fight both shock and loss of blood. Both were equally deadly. I treated for shock then tried to start IVs. All my experience, all my training came into play as I tried to find a vein that wasn't collapsed. But every vein I found was flat. Nonetheless, I managed to get needles inserted and start the flow from the IV bottles.

"Roy, hold this up!" I yelled, handing him the solution bottle. It had to be elevated as much as possible to allow gravity to act. He grabbed the bottle, held it aloft, then just as the solution began to dribble down the tube, a sniper opened up, shattering the bottle in his hand in an explosion of glass and mist.

"Jesus," exclaimed Hoatland, dropping his arm. "Give me another!"

I stuck a fresh bottle on the tube and handed it back. Again, as soon as he raised it the sniper fired. The bottle shattered.

"Goddamned rice burners!" cursed Roy. "Let's try it again!"

Again I jammed a bottle on the tube and gave it to Roy. It lasted as long as the first two. "This won't work. You're gonna get your arm blown off!"

There was only one other thing I could try. I put the IV tube in my mouth and blew. The contents ran down the clear plastic tube and entered the vein. I refilled the tube from a fresh bottle and blew again. It worked. Over and over I repeated this. But it was no use. Two hours later, still filling and blowing through the tubes, the two Marines died.

An hour later, the ambush ended. The Marines had fought the NVA off, then regrouped to pick up the pieces of what remained of Mike Company. We had lost twenty-three men. Twenty-three guys that I had bandaged, sewn up their cuts, treated their jungle rot, listened to their problems and shared their humor and their misery. They were my family. Now they were gone.

145

As the medevac choppers pulled off I sat down and began to cry as the grief and frustration overwhelmed me.

"Let it go, Doc."

I looked up. It was Hoatland. "I can't," I sobbed. "So many good men . . ."

"I said, let it *go*. You did everything you could. We all did. Now let's get out of here."

There was something in his words, something in his manner that made me feel better. I couldn't change what had happened, and the loss haunted me, but Hoatland's words brought me back to reality. There would be more operations, more patrols, and more actions ahead where the men of Mike Company—at least what remained of it— would need me. Faithful old "Doc Tim." That's who I had to be. In this land of death, I had to serve the living. I picked myself up, shouldered my gear and joined the company. But I mentally changed our nickname from "Mad Mike," to "Medevac Mike."

The patrols around Con Thien began to blend with each other in repetitive nightly drudgery. Combat was not a daily thing, but came often enough to keep you off balance and break any welcome monotony. By the end of July, the memory of the ambush in Leatherneck Square had been locked away in the back of my mind like a movie I had seen too often and only took out on occasion. The memory never completely left—it never would—but I had become hardened.

We were moving up the road, back toward Con Thien after an all-night ambush patrol, when it occurred to me that I was getting short. My time in the bush was drawing toward a close and this was the day my replacement was scheduled to arrive. As we marched in two columns, one on each shoulder of the road to avoid any mines that might have been planted overnight, I looked ahead toward the gate to the compound. There, in the distance I could see a jeep with two men sitting in it watching us approach. As we drew closer, I could see that one of them was my replacement.

It wasn't going to be that easy. Nguyen of the North hadn't quite finished with Doc Tim. Before we could enter the safety of the compound and the bunkers therein, I heard a familiar sound.

"Incoming! Incoming!" screamed NCOs as troops scrambled off the sides of the road. I dove for cover, but was too slow. Rockets screeched in, impacting up and down the road. I felt myself lifted and cast through the air like a piece of debris. Slamming to the ground, I rolled into a shallow depression and began checking for damage. Though only four rockets were fired, the platoon took casualties. And this time, one of them was me. I had taken shrapnel in my foot and ankle, but could still get around. I crawled to another Marine, a private named Kelly, who had taken shrapnel in his back and kidney, and began working on him. That completed, I wrapped a couple of battle dressings around my own foot, got to my feet and hobbled toward the main gate.

The BNG (Brand New Guy) who was to replace me stared with eyes wide in shock. He had seen the whole thing and now stood there, gaze transfixed on the dirty, raggedy bunch of grunts with shrunken frames, hollow eyes and battle dressings now entering the gate. His face was ashen with apprehension as he watched each man pass.

I thought back to when I had first arrived and how, when I first received my draft notice, I had done everything I could to stay out of the infantry. I thought of the fears I had held of being killed or maimed and of how I had changed over the months I had spent with Mike Company. I felt mixed relief and pride for having made it.

As I limped by I fought back the urge to reassure him. Instead, after so many months of paying my dues, and feeling his turn was coming, I half-grinned, put on my best "war face," and said: "Just another day in Vietnam."

22

Medics with Green Berets

President Nixon felt by 1970 that the conflict in Southeast Asia could not be won by purely military means. He and Henry Kissinger both believed that a combination of firepower and diplomacy would have to be used to bring about a compromise peace that would allow America to exit from Vietnam to achieve his campaign promise of "Peace with honor."

It would take military successes to buy time for diplomacy to work and for Vietnamization to succeed. In April, the U.S. forces and ARVNs invaded Cambodia, swept the Parrot's Beak and Fish Hook regions and generally created havoc with the communists. But it was also in April that Hanoi had a similar plan carried out. In isolated areas, NVA regiments crossed the border of Cambodia and Laos to strike at thinly garrisoned outposts manned by a handful of American Special Forces troops and their local indigenous counterparts. The A Team that formed the American element of these camps consisted of specialists cross-trained in two or more fields. Each could do the job of another should the necessity arise. The SF medic was no exception.

More than a medic trained to work with the infantry as the primary lifesaver, an A Team medic's job encompassed many responsibilities. Since the A Team camps were normally located in isolated areas, and usually co-located with friendly villages, the SF "Doc" was required to function not only as the local medic capable of patching up and evacuating the wounded, but as a surgeon, dentist, laboratory technician, veterinarian and camp sanitation supervisor. Then, if the situation called for it, he had to be able to use the radio, fire all the weapons, call in an air strike or medevac and even lead a patrol or an attack.

For this, he was not only trained as a medic, but also cross-trained in at least two other skills. Before he was allowed to attend his Special Forces training at Fort Bragg, he had to successfully complete thirty-five weeks of medical training at Brooke Army Medical Center at Fort Sam Houston, Texas. Upon graduation, he was sent on to the next phase: more medical training at Fort Bragg. Here, he learned to perform minor surgery, reset compound fractures, and treat gunshot wounds and tropical diseases. For these tasks, he is issued an aid kit much more elaborate than the infantry medics. Then, when deployed, he had to be ready to function as an instructor to teach his counterpart medics of the local population the skills necessary to assist and, if need be, take over the medical responsibilities of the camp.

To escape the liberal campus environment of an eastern university, Gary Beikirch enlisted in the army with three goals in mind: get into Special Forces, become a medic, and go to Vietnam.

"In 1967 the war in Vietnam was beginning to infect the attitude of the American public, especially those on college campuses where the conflict was the topic of almost every conversation. As a college student at a very liberal university, I saw what the news media called 'campus unrest' almost every day. Controversy prevailed on my campus. People protested against the war, against the bombing and against the draft at every opportunity. I had mixed feelings. I didn't like the thought of killing people, but my country was involved in a situation that called for the youth of America to pick up the gauntlet as our forefathers had in wars of the past. I was curious about Vietnam and I was burned-out on school. How could you protest something you had no firsthand knowledge of?

"I had read a book called *The Green Berets* by Robin Moore, an author who had gone over and worked with the early Special Forces units. It piqued my curiosity about the war and spiked my interest in Special Forces. It was a new direction to explore. I wondered if I too could be a Green Beret. Armed with this newfound interest, I visited the Army Recruiting Station.

"It was then that I found out that you couldn't enlist in the Green Berets. The recruiting sergeant explained that *if* I successfully completed several other phases of training, including Airborne, I could apply. More specifically, *they* would find *me* sometime during or after Jump School and I could apply then. No guarantees. But if that's what it took, so be it. I enlisted.

"I began to worry after basic training. My MOS of Airborne-unassigned became Light Weapons—Infantry, *assigned.* My hopes of wearing the Green Beret began to fade until I received orders for Jump School at Fort Benning. Then when I arrived at Jump School, I found that my class had Recon Marines, Navy SEALs and guys planning on going SF. One day during the training, some guys came down from Fort Bragg wearing Green Berets. I studied them with envy. They looked sharp, intelligent and mature. Quite a contrast from the average young soldiers, most of whom were draftees, I had been around since basic. Then they made an announcement.

"'Those of you who think you have what it takes for Special Forces will undergo more testing. The tests will include aptitude and physical tests. Those qualifying will report to Fort Bragg for training at the Special Warfare School. Anyone who thinks they want to give it a shot give your name to your first sergeant.'

"My chance had finally come.

"I passed all the tests and was selected. My first goal had

been accomplished. But then, my second goal seemed to fade when I was called into the instructor's office.

" 'Your aptitude is not in the medical field, Beikirch. Your strength, according to the aptitude tests is in light weapons.'

"My hopes again bottomed out. I pleaded. I argued. Finally I begged. 'But I want to be a *medic.* I'll do whatever is necessary to become qualified. Just give me a chance and I won't let you down.'

"The instructor thought a moment then smiled. 'Okay, Beikirch, tell you what we'll do. We'll start you in medic training on a trial basis. Screw it up and you'll be humping weapons,' he warned.

"I didn't want to hump weapons. I also didn't realize what I had just gotten myself into.

"Special Forces medical training was eighteen months long. A year-and-a-half after starting the training I had had schools that qualified me to do everything from dentistry to surgery. Taught by army doctors, we learned how to do surgical procedures, fill teeth, prescribe drugs, diagnose diseases, analyze blood and do other laboratory procedures, and even treat animals. We would be working in a field environment on our own and outside medical support would often be out of reach. We had to be able to do it all. This was followed by ten weeks of on-the-job training in an army hospital, rotating through each section to gain hands-on experience. Two weeks of this was in the emergency room and would prove the most important phase of this training in the months to come. Especially important here was the amount of suturing and minor surgery we had to do. The training lasted eleven hours a day, followed by studying at night until lights out. I was glad when it was over.

"The hospital training was followed by another stint at Fort Bragg known as 'dog lab.' In this, each medic was issued a dog to serve as a patient. My thoughts that this would be veterinary training were dispelled when we were told to shoot the 'patient' and then save its life. After each student succeeded in this task, we had to perform various surgical procedures on the animals ranging from tracheotomies to amputations. This was a tremendous experience that would later save a lot of human lives in Vietnam. Though we used anesthesia for pain we were not allowed to use any medications for infection. Instead, we had to use debriding and natural wound healing. After completion of the months of Special Forces medical training, and secondary specialized training in light and crew-served weapons, I was ready for Vietnam."

Beyond the medical training and the required Airborne School, he received training in jungle warfare, demolitions, weapons, psychological warfare and even a foreign language. With all this under his belt, his next stop was Vietnam.

Near the triborder area of Vietnam, where Cambodia, Laos and Vietnam come together, the most vulnerable Special Forces camp in South Vietnam rested in a valley reminiscent of Dien Bien Phu. And the North Vietnamese knew it.

In the first months of 1970, Team A-245, sharing the Montagnard village of Dak Seang, had no way of knowing that they had been targeted by Hanoi for destruction.

23

Sgt. Gary Beikirch
Team A-245, B Company
5th Special Forces
Camp Dak Seang, II Corps
1969-1970

The Montagnards called it "The River Of Blood." That's what *Dak Seang* meant in the local language. When I arrived at A-245, little did I know how the name would become a prediction of our fate.

Unlike the other Special Forces camps that dominated high ground along the border north of us, we were in a valley surrounded by mountains and jungle. Anyone who looked at the place tactically could see that it appeared to have been designed by Custer and was quite reminiscent of Dien Bien Phu—and we all knew what had happened to the French there. And like Dien Bien Phu, we were well entrenched with bunkers, underground rooms, watchtowers, and mortar, 105mm howitzer and machine-gun pits. Around this central compound, several rows of concertina wire circled the camp, dotted with mines, "foo gas" (a mixture of gasoline and napalm jelly in various containers that could be detonated by explosives) and trip wires. Beyond the wire stretched cleared fields of fire. The camp was built in the shape of a square and divided into an inner and outer compound. The outer perimeter included a six-foot deep trench with underground rooms spaced along its length for the Montagnards to occupy. Within the inner perimeter were the underground medical and commo bunkers, the supply shed, a school, the dispensary and the aboveground team house. The "Yards" had learned a lot about fighting an enemy equipped with rockets, mortars and artillery. In the midsixties, a village fifteen miles north of us at Dak Sut had been overrun and all the inhabitants had been massacred. The Yards did not want that to happen again—and neither did we. Everything of a military nature was dug in and fortified.

The security immediately outside the outer perimeter was the responsibility of our twelve LLDB *(Luc-Luong Dac-Biet*—South Vietnamese Special Forces) counterparts, and areas beyond that fell to our Montagnard strikers. The fact that the Yards hated and distrusted the Vietnamese in general and the LLDB in particular made for a few intense encounters. The Vietnamese looked down on the mountain tribes as uneducated savages, and the Yards considered the Vietnamese cowardly lowlanders who knew little of the mountains and forests of the tribal lands of the Montagnards. Buffering these two camp factions were those of us in the Special Forces A Team.

Our mission was threefold: run surveillance missions in our operational sector of the Ho Chi Minh Trail, assist and enlist the aid of the local Montagnards by winning their trust and loyalty, and perform any other needed missions handed down by our support B Team at Kontum or our headquarters C Team in Pleiku. These included serving as a jumping-off point for missions performed by CCC (Command and Control Central) and Mike Force recon teams going across the border. The first two basic missions were integral to each other. With the 2300 inhabitants of Dak Seang village, we had plenty of willing and able help.

As the team medic, my job was much more diversified than that of the regular line company medics serving with conventional infantry units. Besides handling the medical problems of the Americans in the team, I was the *Bac Si,* or doctor, for the village, and served as the camp dentist and even veterinarian for the livestock as well. The main mission of Special Forces was to win the hearts and minds of the indigenous population and each member of the team made his own contribution. The weapons and demolitions specialists trained the indigs in their respective areas of expertise, and I both treated the Montagnards and taught them how to take care of themselves and each other. Much of my work concerned their well-being and health. For this, they were extremely grateful and loyal. I grew to love and respect them and they reciprocated in kind. I was very happy at Dak Seang and felt fortunate at having been assigned to an A Team. But going to an A Team was not something that happened to new SF troopers just out of training. First, one had to pay some dues. And I had paid mine.

It was July 1969 when I first arrived in Vietnam at Cam Ranh Bay. Cam Ranh was by then a sprawling military installation checkerboarded with permanent buildings, roads, a seaport and an airfield. Military personnel of every description hustled about doing myriad rear echelon tasks. Replacements arrived every day to fill the voids in field units created by rotations and body bags. Clerks and NCOs punched typewriters and filled forms that dictated men's fates like worker bees in a massive hive following directions from an unseen queen bee. In this backwater of army bureaucracy I would have become a lost soul had it not been for my medical background. All my training, coupled with my rank of Spec Four, paid off with a distinguished position with the occupational skill of shit burner. Each day found me dragging cans of human excrement out of latrines, pouring diesel oil on top of the putrid mess, then torching it to kill the maggots. After the fuel burned down, I stirred it with a stick, added more oil and repeated the process. All my medical training had been reduced to this. Sanitation duty.

Things just weren't working out the way I had planned when I volunteered for the army almost two years before. Instead, every time I had set a goal, fate would attempt to keep me from achieving it.

One day, as I was diligently occupied in raising my body count of fly larvae, a voice called out behind me.

"What are you doing there?"

I turned. The first thing that caught my eye was the beret on the head of the speaker—then his rank. "Burning shit, Sergeant Major."

He studied my beret. "Put that stick down and come here."

"I guess this is Vietnam, huh?" I asked as I approached, wiping my hands.

"This ain't Vietnam. Follow me."

As we walked he told me that he was a sergeant major who worked with CCC working out of Kontum. I explained that I was new in-country, a medic, and was looking for a home.

"Well, we happen to need medics up where I'm at. I'll get you out of here to Nha Trang. When you get there, you request FOB Two at Kontum. When you get to Kontum, come over to see me at CCC. I'll take it from there."

My salvation had arrived. Within a few days I was on my way to the war.

All the SF medics had to spend time in a C Team hospital before being assigned to the field. My assignment took me to Pleiku. Across the street from the CIDG (Civilian Irregular Defense Group) hospital was the compound for the Mike Force—the mobile reaction force whose mission was to reinforce any SF camps under siege. I was fascinated by the activity going on around me and watched the Mike Force people with envy. They were well trained, highly motivated and well led. *These* guys went into *combat. That* was where I belonged. But before I could request transfer, combat came to Pleiku. Rockets shattered the calm night and burst within

156

the camp in blinding flashes of light, bringing me my first experience of battle—and my first battle casualty.

Calls for medic drifted across the camp and I was soon out with my aid bag to lend assistance. A Vietnamese guard had been hit by shrapnel that had blown off the back of his skull. He was in bad shape. Even though I felt there was not much I could do, I worked over him to get him ready for medevac. Maybe in the hospital the surgeons could do more. But it was a losing battle. Within minutes he was dead. This event was my first exposure to combat and its impact was something I would never forget. Even though I had failed to save this man, I felt that in most situations where there was a reasonable chance for survival I *could* save lives. I knew then I had to get to the field where people needed my skills on a continuous basis. Within a few days I went to the C Team command post and asked for transfer to Mike Force.

"That's fine, Biekirch, but first I think you should go out and work some of the camps. You'll get some valuable experience out there. Then if you still want to go to Mike Force, we'll see what we can do," said the sergeant at headquarters.

This turned out to be a lucky break and good advice. I spent a few weeks traveling around to the various camps in II Corps and getting my feet wet working with the A Teams. I grew to love all the guys in the bush and was taken with their mission: The A Teams worked with the people.

The fierce Montagnard tribes of the hills were a simple people, but very loyal and honest. I was struck with the beauty of the highlands and felt at home with the A Teams. Everyone I ran into, from the SF troopers to the Yards, wanted me to stay and be their "Doc." In comparison to the time I had spent knocking around from school to school in the States and being shuttled between various duties after arriving in Vietnam, it was like finally finding long-lost friends. Instead of just one tour, I decided to spend the remaining four years of my enlistment in Vietnam working with the Montagnards. I felt like a missionary who had just been offered his first foreign mission. When it came time to choose my permanent location I returned to the C Team with my mind made up. I requested assignment to an A Team and my request was granted. My new home would be Team A-245 at Camp Dak Seang.

Dak Seang was a small camp three miles from the Laotian border, seventy miles southwest of Da Nang. Bracketed by the SF camp of Ben Het to the south and Dak Pek to the north, Dak Seang fell into a strategic area in what is called the "triborder" area where Laos, Vietnam and Cambodia come together. The NVA using the Ho Chi Minh Trail needed access, like a funnel, through this area to infiltrate the Central Highlands. It was our job to keep an eye on this entry point.

Led by Capt. Paul Landers, the team consisted of eleven Americans including an executive officer, light and heavy weapons specialists, a demolitions specialist, a communications specialist and me. I quickly found that a small team whose very survival depended upon each man doing his job had no room for friction or cliques. An A Team is a family, and as such, friendships quickly develop and acceptance of a new man becomes almost automatic. Sgt. Pat "Dizzy" Dizzine, our commo man, and Sgt. Gordy "Rock" Wiley, a weapons specialist, quickly adopted me and showed me the ropes.

Incorporated with the A Team camp was the village of Dak Seang. It was inhabited by the Sedang, a fierce tribe of Montagnard mountain warriors. The Sedang were a gentle and basic people, but were capable of being both extremely loyal to their friends and fiercely aggressive to their enemies. They considered themselves completely separate from the Vietnamese and their government, occupying tribal lands going back thousands of years. And with this ancient culture came ancient beliefs and customs. Though influenced by various Christian missionaries, they still held to many tribal beliefs and rituals.

I grew close to these people quickly. With our main job being to help them in any way we could, I found myself participating in such activities as building a swimming hole at a nearby river for the kids, showing outdoor movies dropped off by the weekly supply choppers, improving the camp health and sanitary conditions and treating the local livestock. But even with these modern influences, the Sedang still clung to many ancient teachings and traditions. Yet, they also were not afraid to allow modern technology to come to their aid when necessary. This was the case when Chom, one of my Montagnard medics, appeared at the dispensary one day carrying his six-month-old daughter in his arms. By the expression on his face I could see that he was greatly troubled. Several members of his family stood behind him, concern also showing on their faces.

"What's the matter, Chom?" I asked.

"*Bac Si,* my daughter is very sick. Can you help her?" he asked, laying the child on the table.

"Let me take a look." I examined the child and noted a high fever, dehydrated body and other symptoms of disease. I would have to run some tests to isolate the cause of the fever. My dispensary was fully equipped with laboratory equipment and included all the necessary items required to do blood workups and cultures including a microscope and centrifuge. I explained what was necessary and drew some blood.

"How long has she had this fever?" I asked as I worked.

"One week, *Bac Si.* Can you make her well?"

"I'll try, Chom. First I have to see what the problem is."

The family gathered around and settled in for a long wait. They would stay if it took all night, and it would. It lasted beyond the night. Over the next three days I took several specimens, analyzing each in turn to see if there was anything different in each that would give a clue to the cause of the ailment. Each day her condition worsened. Finally I found a strain of protozoa—falciparum.

"It's malaria," I informed Chom. "I can now give her medicine." I felt good knowing that I had the solution to the problem. Chom was my number two medic and a very good friend. It was very satisfying to know that now I could do something for him and his family. I began treatment for malaria.

I retrieved a vial of chloroquine from the medical supplies and filled a syringe with the proper dosage, then reduced the dosage below that needed for the baby's size and weight. I normally mixed medicine in Dimetapp elixir for oral dosage, but the malaria in this case was so advanced that I decided to use an injection instead. I double-checked the dosage and gave the injection.

Immediately things turned from bad to worse. The child had a negative reaction and went into anaphylactic shock that would cause dilation of the blood vessels, constriction of the bronchial tubes—and death. She was having an allergic reaction. I grabbed our anaphylactic tray, built-up for just such an emergency, and went to work. I administered Benadryl and epinephrine in accordance with the required dosage, but still no positive reaction. Now I became scared. I was losing her. I tried a sodium carbonate injection, and then mouth-to-mouth resuscitation and heart massage. I tried everything I could think of. Still no response. The family watched in silence as I worked.

I wracked my brain trying to come up with something else to do, but to no avail. I felt a hand on my shoulder.

"Bac Si," said Chom, "it's okay."

I felt myself overcome with grief. My confidence was shattered. I had tried everything I knew and had failed. How could they accept this so easily? I had let them down when they needed me. Did the little girl die because of my efforts or in spite of them? Questions raced through my mind. What else could I have done? Did I do something wrong? I did everything I was trained to do but had lost. Yet, as so often happens in the mountains, the family accepted the things that could not be changed. I couldn't. I knew that in the weeks to come I would do anything necessary to save Montagnard lives. Their trust and friendship demanded it. I owed it to them.

In the following months I had many chances to make amends for the little girl's death. Battle casualties came in requiring wound treatment, surgery and even amputations. Other cases from the village arrived that needed treatment for snake bites, and even one Yard was brought in that had been mauled by a tiger. Those I could not handle locally I triaged for medevac. I accompanied patrols and company operations, handled wounds caused by everything from gunshots to booby traps, and participated in missions ranging from ambushes to seismic sensor recovery. But the most unusual case that came to my attention concerned not a battle casualty but a curse.

Though the Sedang had been influenced by French Catholic missionaries, the tribe had a witch doctor—a wizened little shaman who practiced the black arts right out of the Stone Age. He held great power over the minds of a people steeped in an ancient culture that believed in the power of demons and spirits. In their minds, everything in the world had a spirit. Mountains, trees, rivers, animals, even rocks had spirits—and spirits could be called upon and influenced if you knew the secrets. People also had spirits. And spirits could be cursed.

I had a good relationship with the witch doctor, developed as soon as I had arrived. He had his area of responsibility and I had mine. Basically, if he couldn't cure someone, he brought them to me. But one patient came not because he was referred but because he had ticked off the witch doctor.

Yoih was one of our assigned bodyguards. The Montagnards assigned certain men to serve as security for the Americans in the camp, and Yoih, along with another Yard, took good care of me. He came to me one day complaining of weakness, diarrhea, dehydration and an inability to keep food down.

"What's wrong, Yoih?" I asked as I started my examination.

"The witch doctor has put a spell on me."

"What?" I asked, amused at his primitive belief.

"A spell, *Bac Si*. I am going to die."

"That's ridiculous, Yoih. He has no power over you. There's got to be something else the matter with you."

I continued my examination, looking for signs of cholera or the liver condition indicated by his jaundiced appearance, but could find nothing apparently wrong. The symptoms were too diversified to be caused by just one disease.

161

It baffled me. Finally I concluded that he was suffering from a psychosomatic belief in the power of the curse, but I did not want to take any chances. Finally his family made him leave their bunker from fear of the spell's being contagious.

I decided to observe him for a few days to monitor any signs of improvement or decay in his condition. He came to sick call every day and his condition worsened. I decided to medevac him to Pleiku. After a week of IV, blood work, every modern treatment possible, he died. No one in Pleiku could determine what was wrong with him either.

The Yards swore it was the voodoo.

But Yoih's death, in a bizarre way, would save many lives—including mine.

24

The Calm Before the Storm

For several days in the last two weeks of July 1970, the North Vietnamese Army infiltrated the mountains and jungles around Dak Seang with regiments of infantry and artillery. Rocket launchers were set up under camouflage cut from the surrounding jungle, mortars were emplaced within range of the camp and registered on priority targets, and the entire camp was placed under surveillance by NVA scouts and officers.

Every aspect of the camp's defenses was studied. All plans would have to be made from what was available from reconnaissance reports. Since this was a Montagnard camp, it would be impossible to infiltrate with spies. The Montagnards would know who belonged inside and who didn't and would deal harshly with any enemy found within the camp.

But it was not as difficult to gain the needed information as had been expected. The South Vietnamese troops stationed at the camp did not aggressively patrol their area of responsibility, and this made it much easier to get close for detailed observations—and later to provide assembly areas for the assault troops.

For days the camp was watched while preparations were made. Dak Seang, which had interfered far too often with the infiltration routes into Vietnam from Laos and Cambodia, would have to be eliminated. With the massive force that had been brought to bear, Dak Seang must surely become another Dien Bien Phu.

Then the date was set: April 1—in the early morning hours when the camp would still be asleep. It would be a standard attack: 82mm mortars and 122mm rockets followed by massed waves of soldiers hitting the defensive barbed-wire fences—sappers breaking through first with satchel charges followed by squads of AK-47-bearing soldiers. Then as the rocket and mortar barrage lifted it would be a simple matter of overwhelming the tiny American garrison, taking out the isolated strong-points, and annihilating the tiny ragtag mountain tribesmen.

The plan was finalized, the time for the attack set. Now it was only a matter of waiting. . . .

25

Sgt. Gary Beikirch
Camp Dak Seang

Yoih's body was flown back to Dak Seang to be buried. As is the tradition, a feast was prepared, mourners assembled, rice wine dispensed, and a wake ensued in the Montagnard section of the camp. Our team attended out of respect and joined in the ceremony. The funeral was to last all night, then the body buried the next morning. But at three o'clock in the morning the event was interrupted by other, more powerful demons in the form of 122 millimeter rockets and heavy artillery.

Unknown to us, the NVA had managed to surround the camp. The buildup had been taking place for almost a month, with no indication that it was occurring. Their purpose was to eliminate Dak Seang as a threat to their incursions into Vietnam and they were determined. Two NVA infantry regiments and an artillery regiment stood poised in dug-in positions in the jungles and mountains surrounding the camp to overwhelm our tiny garrison. The attack was timed to follow a massive rocket and artillery barrage. When the barrage lifted, the NVA regulars could be expected to hit the wire.

We heard the screech of rockets as they raced toward their targets, followed by the impact of each as it found its mark. The gunners were good. Each position in the camp had been preregistered and many began taking direct hits. Brilliant explosions erupted on bunkers, aboveground installations and wire entanglements. They knocked out our commo tower, the dispensary, both of our 105 howitzers, and the camp generator. Other rockets and artillery rounds hit piecemeal about the compound in search of men caught in the open. Had the funeral ceremony not been in progress, all of us would have been within the impact zone.

The funeral quickly broke up as women and children scurried for shelter and men ran for their assigned defensive positions. As I sprinted toward my station in the medical bunker amid explosions and geysers of dirt, I felt a stinging in my buttocks. I felt the area as I ran. My hand came away bloodstained. Damn!

I made the bunker and assessed the situation. My head Montagnard medic, Tung, wasn't there. I needed him. I grabbed two M-3 medic kits and darted out to find him. As I ran I could see that the place was now littered with bodies, some decapitated from the explosions, others missing limbs. I could easily see they were beyond help and continued toward Tung's bunker where I thought he would be.

When I entered the bunker I found him holding his wife, who had fallen victim to a bursting round. Her head was gone. He cradled her lifeless body, rocking back and forth, sobbing and moaning. I shook him to bring him out of it, but it was no use. He was stupefied in his grief and would be of little use. I shared his sorrow, but others needed help and wouldn't wait. I left his bunker and went to the next where I might find Pher, my number two medic.

Pher was there, but had been hit, and suffered a gaping chest wound. I couldn't do anything for him with what I had. I had to find something to seal his chest—something airtight. The wound was too big for a battle dressing package to cover. The seal had to be very large. I remembered the plastic bags that sealed the 105 howitzer rounds when they were shipped. One of those bags would work. I left the bunker and ran toward the supply shed to find one.

Deo, one of my security guards, saw me.

"Bac Si, over here!" he called.

I ran to his side to find another wounded Yard lying on the ground. As I dropped to my knees to examine him, the sky became filled with illumination flares that cast a gray-white light across the landscape, temporarily pressing back the darkness of the night. I glanced up and realized for the first time how serious our situation was. I could now see NVA soldiers hitting the wire in waves. Dirt was being kicked up by small arms fire everywhere. Tracers crossed the compound in brilliant green and white trails, ricocheting off concrete bunkers. The dead, the dying and the wounded were everywhere. I turned back to my casualty. My duty was to the wounded. I had to trust the Yards to fight off the NVA.

That's when I heard it. Sounding like a freight train from hell, a 122 millimeter rocket dropped in its trajectory and seemed to head straight toward me. I flung my body over the casualty to protect him. We were caught in the open between the medical bunker and the school building, with the school being only twenty-five feet away. The round hit the school in a massive explosion. I was picked up and flung through the air, tumbling head over heals, striking the bunker wall. I fell to the ground feeling like I had been kicked in the back by a horse. The pain was excruciating.

I tried to get to my feet but my body wouldn't cooperate. I couldn't move my legs. I had taken a piece of shrapnel across my lower back, striking my spine, and was paralyzed from the waist down. I crawled on my elbows back to the Yard, but he was dead, torn apart by the shrapnel. I knew Pher would be dead by now too. I began painfully crawling toward the medical bunker.

The LLDB had not done their job. They had gone out each day but had not aggressively patrolled their area of responsibility. The NVA had dug tunnels right up to our wire and, as the barrage slackened, came out like rats out of holes. Hundreds emerged and hit the wire, firing AK-47s and B-40 rockets. Several got through and began darting about the compound, inflicting casualties at every opportunity. But the Sedang were fighters and refused to give up an inch of ground without a battle. They were holding, but the situation was perilous.

I finally made the entrance to the medical bunker and slid in. Inside were several casualties and some of our guys, doing what they could to treat the wounded. Pat Noonan, a new medic who had arrived only three days earlier, was bewildered at the instant hell that had taken over Dak Seang, but was pitching in with the wounded. Captain Landers was also there, helping in any way he could. Then he saw me.

"Noonan, take care of Gary!"

Pat looked at me, shock on his face. "Man, you're in bad shape. We gotta get you out of here."

"No, there's too many wounded still out there. Give me a hand and help me get back outside so I can help them." There wasn't any way anyone could get out of Dak Seang with the battle raging, and even if we *could* get a medevac in, there were worse cases than me that would have to go first. I could see no reason for lying around the medical bunker waiting for morning when I could be helping people outside instead.

Faithful Deo pulled me up, put my arm around his shoulders and started for the door. Outside, things were crazy. Incoming were still striking the compound, NVA darted about looking for prey, Montagnards shot repeatedly at moving forms in the dark, machine guns spat angry bursts in long deadly strings, and men screamed and fell as they were struck.

Overlooking all of this was our "John Wayne" tower, a tall structure mounting a .50 caliber machine gun. Our new XO (Executive Officer), who had only been on-site for a few days, was up there firing the machine gun. As I marveled at the sight, a B-40 rocket made a direct hit on the tower, taking it out in a burst of smoke and flame and knocking the XO out onto the ground below. Deo and I crawled to him.

I grabbed an arm to drag him back. The arm moved but the XO didn't. It had been severed from his body. I dropped the arm, grasped his clothing and began dragging him back to the medical bunker. Once inside, I began gathering more supplies. It would take quite a lot to do what had to be done outside.

"Beikirch, you need to stay down here. You don't have any business out there in your condition."

"No way. I've got to get back to those guys outside."

Deo and I exited once again and started making rounds. Another medic, Tot, joined us and took my other arm. Suspended between these two gallant warriors, I moved from man to man applying a battle dressing here, a tourniquet there, anything that was needed.

We returned again to the medical bunker for more supplies and Tot and Deo laid me on the floor.

"*Bac Si,* you need to stay down here," said Tot.

"No."

"But, *Bac Si . . .*"

"I'm going out," I said, and began crawling toward the door.

"Well, if you must go out, we'll go with you."

They came to my side, grabbed my arms, and again we went back into the inferno. Maybe it was a subconscious guilt concerning the dead baby I treated for malaria, maybe it was the trust and friendships I had developed with these gentle backward people, maybe it was a simple call to duty. I don't know. But something drove me on. I *had* to help. I *had* to do what I could to save lives. All about me the Yards were fighting for their lives—and ours. I owed it to them. It was a simple matter of what had to be done at that given moment.

We made our way around the perimeter, tending the wounded, distributing ammunition and doing anything we could to help the defenders. When we came to a bunker that contained a .30 caliber machine gun that was silent, we entered and put the gun back in action, firing into the wire and stacking up NVA until we ran out of ammo.

We exited to find the LLDB lieutenant running around crying like he had been wounded. I pulled him to me and checked him quickly. He was not injured, but he kept crying and crying. I told him to shut up and fight. I harangued him incessantly, but it did no good. He was useless.

I didn't have time to waste on him. Deo, Tot and I left him

to his misery and started out along the perimeter once more. As we found more wounded, we dragged them back to the medical bunker. Each time, we loaded up on more supplies and ammunition and went back to the shrinking perimeter. Finally, after one trip back to the bunker, I was placed on a stretcher covered with blood. I lay there for a few minutes trying to sort things out in my mind and a thought came to me that overwhelmed my consciousness: *If I'm going to die, I'm not going to die down here!*

I began crawling back toward the door. No one was going to stop me. Outside I could hear helicopters—must be the medevacs. The first Huey appeared in the dark, coming over the horizon like a giant dragonfly. As I watched, it burst into a ball of flame and fell into the jungle. A second ship tried to make it in and fell to the same fate, shot down before it could reach us. My heart sank. I felt bad about the fate of the crews that gave their lives trying to reach us. But I had to put the grief aside. There were still too many people that needed me.

I don't know how many trips I made outside. Each trip began to blur and run together with the next. On one trip I returned to the bunker to find a crisis occurring in the operating room. Pat was operating on a severely wounded man who was bleeding profusely. I crawled into the OR to see if I could help.

"I can't get these bleeders stopped!" Pat yelled. "Can you give me a hand?"

Deo and Tot held me up while I worked. First one, then another, I found and tied off the bleeders. Finally, the patient was stabilized. "Think you can take it from here?" I asked.

"Yeah, I think so. You're not going back out there, are you?"

"Yeah. I've got to."

"You can't. You've got internal bleeding. We've got to get you out of here."

During one of our excursions Deo and I had rounded the corner of a bunker and come face-to-face with a couple of NVA. They raised their AK-47s and fired a burst at us just as Deo jerked his M-16 up and squeezed his trigger. Both of them went down, but I felt a pain in my side. I had taken a round through my right side, exiting through my abdomen. My abdomen began slowly filling with blood. I patched myself up as well as I could and kept going, but the guys in the bunker tried to keep me from leaving each time I came back. I knew I could still function and there were worse cases still out there who needed me. *If I'm going to die, I'm not going to die down here. . . .*

Outside, NVA bodies covered the wire. Other NVA ran over the bodies, using them as breaching points, and charged into the inner camp. Dawn had finally come and in the light of day I could see bodies everywhere. Pockets of Montagnards fought valiantly on, mowing down the waves of attackers as they came into range. The darkness of the night was the enemy's ally, the day his foe. The NVA finally pulled back after suffering not only our resistance but the strikes of B-52s and the Vulcan cannons of "Puff." Their mission of annihilation was unfulfilled.

Estimates later showed the NVA force to number over ten thousand men. Against our small garrison of thirteen Americans and two thousand five hundred Yards, half of whom were women and children, this should have been sufficient. But it wasn't. They had underestimated the courage and ferocity of the lowly Montagnards—a people they considered vastly inferior. Their mistake cost them in blood. On the wire alone, one thousand five hundred dead NVA soldiers were left behind. No one knows how many more had been dragged off into the mountains. Unlike Dak Sut and Dien Bien Phu, Dak Seang had held.

I waited on a stretcher for the medevac bird to arrive. Dizzy hovered over me like a mother hen, telling me I would be just fine once I reached the hospital. I tried to pay attention to him but my mind wandered. Then I heard the beating of the Huey's blades as it approached.

I turned my head and saw the green helicopter as it began to descend. Then, just as it came over the distant trees, a massive volume of fire erupted from the jungle. The helicopter banked away and disappeared.

"Oh, my God," I moaned.

"Don't worry, Gary, they'll come back," said Dizzy soothingly. "We'll get you out of here okay."

And it did come back. It took more fire, but this time raced through and landed nearby. Dizzy threw my wretched body on the chopper and stepped back. "See you later, man. Take care of yourself."

As the vibrating machine beat its way into the sky over Dak Seang and banked away toward Pleiku, the crew chief, also a medic, yelled over the noise of the engine and rotors: "You'll be okay now. We'll take care of you."

I settled back and closed my eyes.

When I woke up in the hospital in Pleiku I found myself next to an Australian officer who I knew was one of the company commanders for the Mike Force. He told me that when Dak Seang got hit, they were instantly mobilized. They had boarded Hueys and rushed to reinforce us. But as soon as they had landed in a clearing near the camp they were ambushed. With the exception of him and a few other survivors, his company had been wiped out. But fate has a strange way of catching up with you. After telling me the story, he put his head back on his pillow, gave a sigh—and died.

I was in intensive care. People were dying all around me. It was scary. I wondered if I was also dying. I examined myself and found that I had been catheterized and IVs hung suspended over me, their tubes in my neck. Lower down I saw that an ileostomy had been performed and a large hunk of intestine was hanging out of my abdomen like a bloated snake. The doctors at Pleiku had done all they could for the present. It was now just a matter of time. Either I would make it or I wouldn't.

Over the next two days I faded in and out of consciousness. I remember seeing a few familiar faces during my moments of consciousness. One was Captain Landers, who had been hit and medevacked and now wheeled around the ward in a wheelchair visiting his men. Then a group of officers, all of high rank, arrived from Nha Trang.

"Sergeant Beikirch, tell us what happened out there," said one of the officers.

"Sir?"

"Tell us what happened at Dak Seang. Tell us what you did."

"Well, sir, I just did what I had to. I had a lot of wounded people and did what I could for them." I didn't know if they were writing an after-action report or if I was in some kind of trouble.

"You must have done more than your job. Captain Landers has written you up for the Medal of Honor."

I was speechless. "The what?"

"The Medal of Honor. Just tell us about the battle."

I told them everything I could remember, mentioning all the other guys, including the Montagnards, who did as much as I did, but they kept directing me back to *my* actions. After the interview they flew out to Dak Seang. The investigation was only beginning.

In the coming days I heard nothing more about the Medal. My condition began deteriorating with the onset of pneumonia and postoperative complications. I was worried about my legs. I wondered if I would walk again. But the paralysis proved temporary and feeling was slowly returning to my lower extremities. I began to develop hope, and thoughts of returning to Dak Seang began entering my mind. But any plans of rejoining my team disappeared when the doctors told me that I would go home as soon as I was stabilized. I argued that I could convalesce in-country, that I wanted to stay in Vietnam, all to no avail.

The day finally came and I was sent to Japan, then on to Valley Forge Hospital in Pennsylvania. In October of 1970 I had recovered fairly well from most of my wounds and was returned to duty. But because of my medical profile for permanent disability to my back I could not return to Vietnam. Instead, I was assigned to 10th Special Forces and attached to a headquarters company at Fort Devens, Massachusetts. My attitude began to change. I hated the Stateside army. It wasn't the same. The teamwork atmosphere, the camaraderie, the real-world attitude of the people in Vietnam, were nonexistent here. I didn't want *this* garrison army. If I couldn't go back to *my* army, I wanted out.

I had three years left in this enlistment, but the army was

giving early outs to those wanting to go to school. I decided
to go back to college and try for medical school. I wanted to
become a doctor. With my mind finally made up, I pulled
some strings and in August of 1971 I bid the army farewell.

In my duffel bag were the Silver Star, the Bronze Star, the
Distinguished Service Cross and three Purple Hearts. I had
heard some talk about the Medal of Honor, but that was all.
Now it was time to leave all that behind me and begin the
rest of my life.

Unknown to Gary Beikirch at the time, he had *not* heard
the last about the Medal.

26

The Last Man Killed

On June 16, 1969, the men and equipment of the 1st Amtrac Battalion boarded the landing ship (tank) USS *Iredell County* in Da Nang Harbor. Their next stop would be Okinawa. For them, and shortly for the rest of the 3rd Marine Division, the war was over.

The departure of the amphibian tractor battalion signalled not only the beginning of the 3rd Division's standdown and pullout, but the beginning of America's withdrawal from the war in Vietnam. As each day passed, more and more territory was relinquished to the South Vietnamese forces. Soon, the remaining elements of the 3rd Division would depart, followed by elements of the 1st Marine Aircraft Wing.

But the Marines could not completely withdraw. Not yet. They were still responsible for certain sectors of I Corps until they could be replaced by the ARVNs. The 1st Marine Division, working the areas south and west of Da Nang, continued to hump the paddies and the jungles in the same manner as they had since their arrival in 1966. And as long as they continued to operate, they would receive casualties.

Hospitalman Leonard Finnell had seen the casualties of Vietnam long before he found himself in the jungles of I Corps.

"After Corps School I was ordered to the Naval Hospital at Camp Pendleton. As soon as I reported in I was assigned to the neurosurgery ward where ninety percent of the patients were casualties of Vietnam. Most were head wound cases and many were paralyzed. Working with these guys every day really brought the reality of war home. But in a way, I felt lucky. When I was in Corps School, we were told that half of the class would go to the Marines and if anyone flunked out on purpose to avoid this, they would be sent to Swift boats to shoot machine guns on some river in Vietnam. After two guys flunked out on purpose—and were sent to Swift boats—the rest of us buckled down. I didn't go to Swift boats and so far I hadn't gone to the Marines.

"The strange thing was that I never wanted to be a corpsman. I joined the navy to be a cook. But when my test scores came back the matter was taken out of my hands. I was *told* what I would be and that was that.

"I was really surprised when I ended up at the hospital at Pendleton. I knew that if I stayed there long enough, with all the troop withdrawals and Nixon talking about 'Peace with honor,' that I could do my time Stateside. It didn't quite work out that way. The casualty figures were still high and replacements were still being sent—including corpsmen.

"After seven months at Pendleton we began receiving orders for overseas. One by one my buddies left for various assignments. Most went to ships, or Okinawa, or Japan. This was reassuring. Then my orders came: Field Medical School. I knew what that meant.

"After FMS I was assigned to a line company on Pendleton where I awaited further developments. Two times orders for Vietnam came in and each time they were cancelled. I felt like the guy who gets strapped into the electric chair and before they can pull the switch the phone rings and he gets granted a stay of execution. Then the third set came in and the phone didn't ring.

"On December 30, 1970, I boarded a plane at San Bernardino for WestPac. I was in a state of numbness and nervous anticipation that something awful was happening. The only thoughts on my mind were the patients in the neurosurgery ward—and body bags. There just seemed to be something wrong about going to a war we were in the process of leaving."

On January 4, 1971, ten days after Finnell boarded his flight for Vietnam, Nixon announced that "the end is in sight" for the U.S. combat role in Vietnam. But it wasn't in sight for the men of the 1st Marine Division. For them, "in sight" meant getting on the plane for the trip home. And the most pressing thought on the minds of many of the men who remained, knowing that it was just a matter of time before they would be out of danger, was "I don't want to be *the last man killed.*"

27

HN Leonard Finnell
Bravo Company
1st Battalion
1st Marines
Dai Loc, 1971

I couldn't believe it. I was boarding a helicopter wearing Marine Corps dress greens in the heat of Vietnam—the same dress greens I had put on when I left the States. Everything had been hurry-up. The two-week orientation to prepare us for Vietnam that was to have taken place in Okinawa had not materialized. Instead, when the two-hundred-plus Marines that had flown over with us on the big American Airlines jet deplaned at Kedena Air Base in Okinawa, the corpsmen were told to sit tight. We would be going on to Vietnam on the same plane.

While we waited, other Marines boarded. Only, these Marines, unlike the ones we had crossed the Pacific with, were dressed in battle gear. An ominous feeling settled over the fifteen corpsmen who had flown out of San Bernardino only seventeen hours before. Arrival at Da Nang only deepened the sensation. When I stood from my seat in the air-conditioned civilian airliner and joined the line of troops waiting for the door to open, I couldn't help but note the smiles of the pretty stewardesses as they said good-bye—and Happy New Year. It was January 1, 1971. A hell of a day, and a hell of a way, to go to war.

The door opened, showing the bright light of a clear morning, followed by a distinct odor: the smell of burning shit. *Yeah,* I thought as I moved toward the door, *Happy New Year.*

Outside, the heat was unbearable in our gabardine winter uniforms. It had been cool when we left the States, but it damned sure wasn't here. I stood on the hot tarmac amid dancing heat waves and surveyed the scene while I waited for instructions. The air base was a quiltwork of old and new buildings, parking ramps for aircraft, tents and Quonset huts and dusty roads. Various military vehicles passed, loaded with supplies or troops, leaving clouds of dust in their wake. On the runway, jet fighters loaded with bombs and rockets took off with a thunderous roar and appeared to climb straight up, trailing black smoke as they went. As I scanned this scene of apparent urgency a bus with screen-covered windows drove up and squeaked to a halt next to the plane. As the Marines marched off in one direction, my small contingent of corpsmen boarded the bus. After a short ride we arrived at the division surgeon's office.

"Here're your orders," said the chief at the surgeon's office, passing papers to each man as he answered. "Finnell, you pick up your unit at Dai Loc tomorrow. Catch a helicopter out in the morning."

This was too much. I was incredulous. Things were happening far too rapidly to comprehend. I quickly scanned the orders, then asked, "Chief, what about our two-weeks indoctrination?"

He smirked, then began passing out little booklets titled *Leatherneck Fire Team Phrase Book.* In it were three columns of words. The first column was in English, the one on the far right in Vietnamese, and the one in the middle a phonetic pronunciation for the Vietnamese words. It contained such useful phrases as: "This village is surrounded," and "How many VC are here?"

"That's your indoctrination. The only other thing you need to know is this: You find booby traps two ways, gentlemen. By accident and by accident. And I hope the 'by accident' is the second one, the one where you can walk away." He then looked at me. "That's *very* true for your unit, Finnell. They're the ones who've been in the most shit lately."

That was very reassuring.

The next morning found me climbing into a helicopter still wearing my dress greens, that now stank of sweat, headed for a line company in a place I had never heard of, which specialized in finding booby traps by accident. I still couldn't understand why things were happening so quickly.

I found out when I arrived at Dai Loc and met the corpsmen we were replacing.

"The reason you Docs were rushed over here," said one of the old salts as he handed me his jungle boots, "is because we're expecting a big Tet. Maybe bigger than the one in 'sixty-eight. If the NVA get real brave, we could have quite a few casualties. I'm due to go home, so I won't be needing these anymore."

Another corpsman who had already done his time in the field gave me his canteens, and a Marine from Bravo Company gave me a large NVA rucksack. Someone else gave me a helmet, and another threw me a flak jacket. Before long I had a small mountain of equipment, C rations, fifty pounds of medical supplies, webbing—all the "782" gear the Marines take to the field. Then I was sent to the armorer.

"If you want a rifle, pick one up from a dead Marine. He won't be needing it anymore," said the armorer after handing me a .45 pistol, a holster, four clips and fifty rounds of ammunition. "You'll have plenty of chances."

These words of advice somehow complemented those of the helicopter door gunner's when we had landed on the hill that morning. As I started to crawl through the door he had grinned and said, "If you like action, Doc, here's where you'll find it."

I wasn't looking for action, but somehow I felt that it would find me.

"You our new corpsman?" asked the company commander of Bravo Company, 1st Battalion, 1st Marines.

"Yes, sir."

"Good. I'm going back out to the unit now. You can ride with me."

I shouldered my gear and followed him to the waiting chopper. After a flight that was all too short we landed in the middle of my first jungle at five o'clock in the afternoon. By seven o'clock I was standing my first watch. I was still suffering jet lag, my body felt drained in the intense heat that I'd had no time to become accustomed to, I didn't know any of the twelve people in the squad I was assigned to, I had gone from a cold winter in California to a hot, humid jungle in Vietnam in three days, and it was getting dark. I looked around and wondered whose rifle I would get.

When I'd drawn my two-hour watch, a Marine cocked the M-60 machine gun set up next to me, rolled to one side and said, "Doc, if anything moves on that trail out there, cut loose with the gun." He laid three claymore mine clackers in front of me, their wires trailing off into the dark, and instructed, "Squeeze 'em two times each and they'll go off. In two hours, wake this lance corporal up." He pointed to a sleeping form on the ground nearby. "This ain't the States. We don't get much sleep over here. Two hours means two hours. Not one minute before."

He rolled up in his poncho and went to sleep. I still couldn't comprehend what was happening. But I did know one thing, I was scared spitless.

The night passed uneventfully and I was never so glad to see the sun in my life. Within a few hours we "saddled up" and began the long walk back to the fire support base. Ten miles of trudging beneath the blazing sun brought us back to Dai Loc and a five-day period of escorting minesweeping details, conducting patrols and setting up ambushes. Then on the morning of the tenth I was called to see the platoon sergeant, Staff Sergeant Black. Black was a friendly and easygoing black man who loved the Marine Corps, took good care of his men and exhibited fine leadership qualities at all times. In the coming weeks I would grow to respect and trust him. "Doc, you're going to sit in on the briefing for the next operation. It's not because you're new in-country, but because all the corpsmen sit in on the briefings so they'll know what's coming down. It's policy. This operation could get hairy and I want you ready for it," he explained as we entered the briefing tent.

I took a seat next to Black. In the front of the tent was a large map pinned to a piece of plywood. Several colored lines, arrows and numbers graced its acetate surface. Before the map stood the briefing officer, a crisply dressed lieutenant with a pointer. Finally, when he determined all were present, he spoke.

"Gentlemen, this is Operation Upshur Stream. It will be the first major operation on Charlie Ridge in over a year." He slapped the map with the pointer. Everybody knew Charlie Ridge. We'd even heard of it Stateside. We knew it as "Indian territory." The NVA owned it. No matter what you did, *they* owned it. Though I had only been in Vietnam ten days, I had heard all I wanted to about Charlie Ridge.

The briefing officer continued. ". . . numerous NVA and we're going to take casualties. But we're going to pull this operation off and we're going to kill them. Intelligence says there're all sorts of NVA there now, well dug-in, well supplied, and part of the Ho Chi Minh Trail network that feeds into the Da Nang area. As you know, Bravo Company is down to one hundred and twenty men. So, because of our reduced strength, we're going to be the guinea pig company. Our job is to drive anything before us down into Delta, Fox, and Kilo companies who will be in a blocking position . . . here." Again the pointer hit the map. I didn't like the sound of "guinea pig company."

On January 11, 1971, Operation Upshur Stream started.

The operation began with a good sign: The LZ on the hilltop had been "cold." No one complained about the lack of a reception committee, and after the helicopters pulled away and disappeared in the distance, a quiet calmness settled over the hill. The helicopters were our link to reality, and once they were gone a feeling of loneliness and abandonment, like that of an orphan cast out to fend for himself, permeated the air. But we had no time to dwell on that. Amid shouts from the gunny and the platoon sergeants, we quickly formed up and moved off the hill. Within an hour we entered a dense dark triple canopy jungle infested with snakes, leeches and scorpions. It was hot, humid and stinking. It closed in on us like a shroud, making me feel even more alone, taking away the sense of numbers and allowing me to see only the man in front and the man behind.

We moved fast, carried only what we needed, had all the air support we could use, and had laid on artillery to cover our route of advance. Yet, instead of feeling covered and secure, I was scared. We felt—knew—that we were being watched. There were eyes in the jungle: NVA eyes.

Before long we came across enemy bunkers and tunnels and blew them as they were discovered. It was evident that the NVA had just left. I felt that sooner or later we would run into them—on their terms. They had to be waiting, planning, getting organized.

Our company commander was a mustang officer. He had worked his way up through the ranks and was fearless. Nothing seemed to bother him. Yet when I looked at *his* eyes, I could see that things were just not going the way they were supposed to. I could tell he was nervous. And he was a lot more experienced than I. If the skipper was nervous, I was terrified. As each hour went by the tension mounted. By nightfall, we had still not run into the enemy. Then after a night of apprehension and worry and still no contact, we moved out again. All day we struggled through the jungle, but this day was a repeat of the first. When would the NVA decide to hit us?

On the third day we were moving fast—too fast—along a well-used trail. It was impossible to move fast and be careful at the same time. Our speed and fatigue combined to dull our previous two days' caution and made us careless. My squad was on point when the NVA finally decided to make their move. They had been watching us and had picked their ground carefully. It was a perfect ambush. Within thirty seconds we were on the ground. It was the kind of ambush that was reinforced by booby traps. If you dropped to the trail you hit booby traps. If you broke out to the side of the trail you hit more booby traps. The squad leader was blown out of the kill zone. Other guys hit booby traps and were riddled with shrapnel. It was a miracle no one was killed. When it was over only I and the assistant squad leader remained unwounded. It was a mess. Ten Marines were down. I looked around in shock and could now *see* booby traps. Chicom grenades were rigged with trip wires along the trail's edge and in the bushes all around us. These traps were not meant to kill, only to inflict casualties. And that's exactly what they did. Two men lost legs, others lost eyes and the rest had various shrapnel wounds requiring immediate medevac. As soon as it started it ended. The NVA melted away before we could counter the ambush and give them some payback.

Everyone who could help gave me a hand patching up the worst cases. I applied tourniquets, battle dressings, whatever was needed and as I worked the captain called in for medevac.

"This is Bravo One Actual. I need medevac. We have *many* wounded. I say again, we have *many* wounded. Stand by for coordinates . . ." The captain bent over his map and read off our position. Then, turning away from the radio handset, "Doc, get over here and tell 'em what you've got!"

I ran over and took the handset from the captain. "This is One-Six. I have many wounded—five critical. I say again, five critical." I knew they would have to send more than just a Huey to get all of the wounded aboard.

I looked around to see where the helicopter could land. The trail was in triple canopy jungle and there was no place a chopper could set down. We would have to use the "bullet," a line weighted by a jungle penetrator device that could be dropped through the canopy. But even for this we had to have a small open area below the trees to move the casualties to.

Our Kit Carson scout, Lux, and a couple of Marines began hacking out an area big enough to get the bullet down. But I could tell that some of the guys were so badly mangled that they couldn't hang on to the bullet. Then I heard the helicopter. The big Marine CH-46 troop carrier slowly came overhead and began to hover. As it began lowering the line, it was joined by army Huey gunships out of Da Nang that banked in to provide fire support for the extraction. Machine guns opened up as each nosed over and strafed the jungle around us. The pilot called on the radio.

"What's the situation down there? Over."

"We've got people hurt too bad to use the bullet. We'll have to use the mesh gurney for five of them," I replied.

"Okay, this is a one-shot deal. We're staying right here until everyone is up. Before we leave, the jungle will be on fire. The army guys are just begging for something to shoot at."

I felt reassurance at this and developed an instant respect for that pilot. He had balls. I wanted to get him out of there as quickly as possible and started placing the least serious casualties on the bullet as soon as it was down. As I worked I heard more explosions. The headquarters element had tripped more booby traps. The first sergeant was down along with three other Marines. I now had fourteen casualties. Each was brought to me in turn and treated just enough to make it back to Da Nang. Forty-five minutes later—with the pilot holding a steady hover for the entire time—the last man was pulled out. In one short action our company strength was cut from an understrength 120 men to 106. I now had my M-16.

Though the day dawned bright after a quiet night on Charlie Ridge, it was dark in the jungle. We had had only a few hours of sleep between midnight and dawn and were hungry. We had run out of rations and needed replacements for the men who had been extracted. I needed more medical supplies. My aid bag had been blown away during the ambush, breaking all my IV bottles, and my flak vest had been ripped to pieces. To receive these supplies and troops an LZ would have to be hacked out of the jungle. Men went to work chopping the vegetation away to clear a large enough area to land the resupply chopper. Instead of one helicopter, two were sent. The first contained mailbags, chow and other supplies. The second carried thirty Marines and a corpsman sent to assist me through the rest of the operation.

The first machine made it in and discharged its contents. I watched as it lifted and turned away toward Da Nang. Beyond I heard the second CH-46 approach. Then, through the trees I could see it as it slowly started its approach to the LZ. But before it made the landing zone, three shots rang out from the jungle. I watched in horror as the machine dipped toward the trees, then cringed as the rotor blades struck, throwing green vegetation skyward as the blades thrashed their way into the trees. It rolled to one side, hit the ground and exploded in a huge billowing ball of flame. As we stood there frozen in shock I could hear *thuds* as objects hit the ground around us. The helicopter, among other things, was carrying a large amount of ammunition and the objects showering us like huge raindrops were M-79 grenade rounds. I stood frozen, unwilling to move. But that didn't last long.

Multiple explosions began erupting around the LZ. I dove into a fighting hole with Staff Sergeant Black. The skipper started shouting orders to man defensive positions. If the NVA wanted to hit us, now was the time. The chopper was still burning only a short distance away, and from the screams I could tell that there were several injured survivors. Too much had happened all at once. I was in a state of shock. Black turned to me.

"Well, Doc, it's time we started earning our money." He was so casual about it. His voice had an immediate calming effect on me. And he was right.

As we crawled from the hole I could see Marines setting up a perimeter, machine gunners mounting their M-60s and quickly determining fields of fire, and other troops running my way to help with the wounded. Overhead, Huey gunships darted around in frustration trying to find targets while the first resupply chopper orbited in a wide circle waiting for a chance to serve as a medevac.

It took two hours to find all the wounded. Some had jumped from the burning helicopter on fire and had run away in panic into the jungle. Others lay scattered around the LZ while still others had managed to crawl into the bushes. As I drew near I could see one of the other company corpsmen doing a cut-down on the senior Kit Carson scout's ankle to find a vein for an IV. There was no other way a vein could be found. He was burned over 100 percent of his body.

I found the new corpsman who had come in with the helicopter. I could tell he was the corpsman by the "caduceus" medical emblem that had been on his collar but somehow had gotten twisted around and was now burned and embedded into his scorched back. I sat next to him, overwhelmed with a mixture of frustration and sorrow, and wrote on a medical tag: "Probable naval personnel." I later found that he had only arrived in-country the day before.

In twenty-four hours we suffered five killed and forty-eight wounded. Those of us that remained were exhausted, hungry and demoralized. And it was growing dark.

"Doc," said Staff Sergeant Black, "get some sleep. I'll take your watch tonight."

"Sleep?" I asked, disbelieving what I had just heard. "The whole night?"

"Yeah. We'll need you in the morning. You're gonna be busy."

"Busy?"

"The dead are still here."

I lay back in exhaustion, thankful for the chance to get some much needed rest and gazed once more across the field of death. In the middle of the perimeter five still forms covered by ponchos rested peacefully, guarded by five Marines who would stay up all night—standing vigil over their fallen comrades. I huddled in my poncho and closed my eyes as a cold rain began to fall. But none of us would sleep that night. None but the dead.

28

A Matter of Survival

It had been a long, hard five years for the Marines. Since the initial landings at Red Beach in 1965, they had fought over ground in all of the five northern provinces. And on many occasions—too many—they had fought over the same ground again. Politics, and politicians, had turned what had earlier been described as a "Splendid Little War," into a quagmire of confusion and frustration. Though the National Liberation Front and the North Vietnamese Army lost every battle at great cost, and in every confrontation American fighting men fought valiantly and with honor, the communists were winning the political war on the streets of the cities of America.

Nixon had promised troop withdrawals and an end to the war. But it wasn't over yet. U.S. operations expanded into both Laos and Cambodia in response to massive buildups of the NVA and the communist Pathet Lao. B-52s made "Arc Light" drops of thousands of tons of bombs in Laos alone, but the bombing did little to stop the communists. For "Vietnamization"—turning the war over to the South

Vietnamese forces—to work, the ARVN would have to be left with the upper hand.

Operation Lam Son 719—a name derived from the site of a Vietnamese victory over the Chinese in 1427—was planned to drive twenty-two miles into Laos to Tchepone, a strategic junction of the Ho Chi Minh Trail. Phase I, the American part of the operation, code-named Dewey Canyon II, began January 30. It was successful in securing Route 9 and reestablishing Khe Sanh as a logistic base. In Phase II, Lt. Gen. Hoang Xuan Lam led twelve-thousand ARVN troops into Laos.

The push went well until they were hit from the north by heavy NVA counterattacks. With the ARVN main effort bogged down, and the reinforcing Ranger and airborne fire bases rapidly becoming untenable due to assaults by North Vietnamese PT-76 and T-54 tanks, Xuan Lam changed his plans.

In the longest-range heliborne operation of the war, two battalions of the ARVN 1st Infantry Division were lifted from Khe Sanh directly to Tchepone, joined by the rest of the division after a series of bounds along the route.

Then, instead of the planned clearing operation, the Vietnamese began suffering heavy casualties. Under pressure from the NVA, Lam ordered a withdrawal on March 10. But instead of an orderly withdrawal, it turned into a rout. Only U.S. air power saved the ARVN from extinction. Casualties numbered almost ten-thousand, with the American support forces losing 107 helicopters and 176 crew members. In the words of Henry Kissinger, "The operation, conceived in doubt and assailed by skepticism, proceeded in confusion."

Thoughts that the Vietnamese were ready to take over the role of the Americans became doubtful. Yet, in Paris, the peace talks continued. And in Washington, the plan to pull out had not changed. U.S. troop levels fell from 280,000 to 156,800.

For the Marine units that continued to slog the rice paddies and hump the hills south and west of Da Nang, the war appeared to be winding down in intensity. Even the casualty figures showed a drastic decrease over the previous year as NVA, and what were left of VC units seemed to avoid contact with Americans in anticipation of the eventual pullout.

Casualties in the Da Nang TAOR (Tactical Area of Responsibility) began to come more from mines and booby traps than from ambushes and assaults. Harassing rocket and mortar fire became more of a nuisance than a threat. It was as if the communists were saying: "See? We're still here, and you could still get killed in Vietnam."

And you could. As each minute ticked by, and as each day was marked off "short-timer" calendars, the war for the marines, who knew that only weeks stood between them and their extrication from Vietnam, became a matter of survival.

29

HN Leonard Finnell, USN

With the exception of our senior corpsman, a devout Mormon who refused to participate in any small unit operations and even let his .45 rust so it wouldn't fire, the corpsmen of the company participated in every type of combat operation with the Marine squads we supported. We practiced preventive medicine, and to us that meant carrying our load as combat troops. If we could prevent one of our Marines from becoming a casualty by killing the enemy first, that's what we would do. Combat patrols, ambushes and sweeps all found us joining the grunts with firepower. Our M-16s were not silent and to the weight of our medical supplies was added the weight of grenades and extra ammunition.

The Vietcong and the NVA took great pleasure in singling out certain critical personnel—leaders, machine gunners, radiomen, and especially corpsmen. Our aid bags and other telltale equipment identified us to snipers as lucrative targets. We knew this and our attitude changed quickly from the helpful noncombatant Doc to a die-hard *combat* corpsman. Combat meant fighting and that's what we did. It became a job of treat-and-shoot or shoot-and-treat, depending on the situation.

A feeling of frustration began to fall over the company with each operation. We found ourselves fighting over the same terrain, the same hills, the same rivers, as the Marines had fought over five years before and each year thereafter. Take a hill, then leave. Real estate wasn't something you took and kept as a mark of success and victory or a trophy to be displayed and held with pride. Instead, hills and areas taken were simply names and grid coordinates mentioned in after-action reports and unit histories at a cost of blood spilled and lives lost. The objective was to find and kill the enemy, not to gain or deny him terrain. Maybe it made sense to the generals, but it made no sense to us.

Meanwhile, the NVA tried to avoid contact with the Marines of I Corps. Instead of the massive battles and artillery barrages of 1968, the war returned to the days of 1965 when most of the casualties were inflicted by mines and booby traps. It wasn't as intensive, but to the individual, it was just as costly.

But the mines and booby traps were not the only hazard to the field troops. After the action on Charlie Ridge I developed a massive cyst on my ankle which soon swelled to a size so large that I couldn't wear a boot. After being pulled off the hill I reported to the Battalion Aid Station at Dai Loc, a crude Quonset hut with rudimentary medical facilities.

"We've got to lance your ankle," said the doctor after a brief examination, "and we don't use anesthetics for this."

I couldn't believe it. The pain of the swollen ankle was bad enough, but the thought of undergoing minor surgery without the benefit of a painkiller was devastating. As I lay on the table, the doctor called in four Marines and two corpsmen.

"Lay on him and hold him still," ordered the doctor as he reached for his instruments. I started to protest, but I knew it would do little good. While I was held fast under the weight of six men, the doctor cut my ankle open. In a twentieth-century world we were now reduced to practicing seventeenth-century medicine.

As soon as possible I wanted out of Dai Loc. Though it was a fairly secure area, occasional mortar rounds visited the hill and sporadic probes reminded us that we weren't forgotten by the enemy. It was too hot to sleep in the bunkers and too dangerous to sleep outside. At least in the field you knew where you stood and had a semblance of control over your fate. As we grew restless with base camp routine a reprieve came in the form of marching orders. Bravo Company—or what was left of it—was once again called upon to trade blood for a mention in history books.

Our captain didn't like helicopters. To him, walking was much safer. For the next few weeks, Bravo would hump mile after mile through the areas around Da Nang known as "Mortar Valley," and the "Rocket Belt." These were two rings that circled the air base where the gooks launched their various weapons against Da Nang. Our job was to find them if possible, or at least deny them the chance to fire.

By now we had a new platoon commander. Just the opposite of Platoon Sergeant Black in character and color was Lieutenant White. Lieutenant White presented himself to the platoon with all the finesse of a bad dream.

"I'm going to be the only hero in this unit. I hear that a few of you have been written up for medals. If there are any medals to be awarded, I'm the one who will get them." He then looked directly at me. He had obviously been told that I, along with two Marines, had been written up for the Vietnamese Cross of Gallantry for our actions on Charlie Ridge. "In the past you corpsmen have stayed with the headquarters element. From now on you will stay out with one of the squads. Is that understood?"

"Yes, sir," I replied, almost glad to have orders to stay away from him. What he obviously didn't realize was that in Bravo Company, with the exception of the senior corpsman, the rest of us *always* were out with the squads. After a few more pointed instructions the meeting broke up. As I walked back to my bunker to assemble my equipment Sergeant Black joined me.

"Doc, looks like you'll have to wait to be a hero."

"Yeah. White's got to get his quota of medals first."

"Not that. Word just came down that all the Vietnamese Crosses are going to the army this month."

I looked at him in question. "The army?"

"Yeah. Seems it's their turn."

"That figures," I mumbled. Now there wasn't even enough recognition to go around. We had to take turns getting it, like the supply was scarce. For us, Vietnam was quickly becoming a dangerous ghetto filled with dead-end streets.

The size of our squads began to diminish. Fourteen-man squads were reduced to six-man squads as men rotated home and were not replaced. Lieutenant White took this opportunity to reorganize the platoon, selecting those who had graduated from high school and had a bit of college and putting us in one squad. We apparently were a threat to him as we had more education than the others and could figure out what was going on and subsequently cast a bitch. The "Motley Seven," as we became known, consisted of five unfortunate Marines with an education, Sergeant Black and me. For our sins we drew constant ambush patrols, night after night. We wondered if this was his way of eliminating any would-be heros in one fell swoop should something go wrong.

But we beat the odds. After days of patrolling and nights of setting up ambushes we remained unscathed. Then the game was changed. Bravo was assigned to a *Chieu Hoi* ("I surrender") village comprised of VC and NVA defectors. Other than being *Chieu Hoi* it was a typical Vietnamese village. A lot of women and children but very few men. There were no ARVN units around to watch the place and the task fell to one of our CAP (Combined Action Platoon) units of about two squads' strength.

During the day I treated the villagers as part of our MEDCAP routine, and during the night I went out with ambush patrols to kill the sons and husbands of the villagers as they tried to infiltrate for a visit from their lairs in Arizona Territory and Charlie Ridge. It became a deadly and bizarre game. Almost every night one of our ambush patrols could be heard opening up with a quick volley of automatic weapons fire. Almost every morning we laid out the dead for the villagers to see. As they cried over the bodies of their relatives the ARVN officials, who came each morning in the safety of daylight, used this show of emotion as a form of identification and arrested them for being enemy collaborators. By "protecting" the village we made enemies of the people we protected.

We continued to expand our patrols throughout the Rocket Belt and inflicted many more casualties on the Vietcong than they inflicted on us. Our small unit tactics were successful if you counted success by body count. Fighting the VC proved quite different from fighting the NVA. The VC were no match for us. Yet our frustration grew with the way the war was being conducted. We knew that we were scheduled to go home in the near future, though we didn't know exactly when. Instead of finding and killing the enemy, our objective became survival. Like those who came before us, we knew that the powers-that-be would not let us win the war in the way we had been trained and motivated to do. And because of this, like the enemy, we began to sense a need to avoid contact. No one wanted to get killed or wounded for nothing. And no one *damned sure* wanted to be the last man killed before we went home.

The army began to arrive around Da Nang in force as the Marines were being thinned out on rotation. The more I saw of them the more I was amazed at the difference in support the army and Marines received from the military system. One day an army infantry unit came by.

"Hey, Doc," I called, spying their medic by his abundance of medical equipment, "got anything you can spare?"

"Maybe. What've you got to trade?"

"I've got a picture of a dead NVA here."

"Okay. What do you need?" he asked, pulling off his medical pack. I named a few items and made the trade. There were two systems of supply in the Marines: the official one that provided very little if anything, and the unofficial one where everyone traded for what they needed. The second worked best and there was no paperwork. For these new army units arriving around Da Nang, "body shots" were quite a novelty, and for a few, I could get just about anything they had. It was a good thing that I stocked up on medical supplies when I did, thanks to my army counterparts. We didn't know it but Operation Peach Orchard was about to begin.

"G-2 (Intelligence) reports that there's an area that the NVA are going to take a group of POWs through in the next couple of days," said the captain. "Our job is to get into that area, stop the NVA and get the prisoners back. Every Marine combat unit left in Vietnam is going to be on this operation and we'll have two ARVN units go in with us as well."

Our company was down to less than a hundred people—less than half our authorized strength. What other services might call combat ineffective the Marines called, "cut-down and fast moving."

The captain continued. "We'll be the chase company. We're going to move hard and we're going to move fast. We'll be lifted in by choppers and go straight into the bush. If there're POWs there, we're going to do our best to find them. Any questions?"

There were none.

The helicopter flight on the big CH-53s lasted much longer than any flight we had been on before. We flew for what seemed like hours. Thoughts of working near, or even across, the border of Laos entered our heads. Finally we began to circle and descend. As the lumbering machines settled onto a hilltop I could see that the entire top of the hill had been blown away by artillery that had been hauled in specifically to prepare it for a landing zone. As soon as our machine touched down, we hit the ground running, spread out and sprinted into the jungle.

It was a strange, eerie world of double canopy jungle. Rays of sunlight only occasionally penetrated the thick vegetation in stabbing beams, marking a tiny opening in the overhead growth like a bullet hole in a tin roof. The heat was overpowering, the air almost too thick to breathe. The damp stink of rotting undergrowth surrounded us and attacked our nostrils with every breath. Under the weight of our combat loads we pressed on, each step reminding us of our weakened conditions. Dysentery had taken its toll among the company. Many carried more weight in equipment and ammunition than their shriveled bodies weighed. I knew I would have to watch for heat casualties—if we didn't run into the NVA first.

As I followed the thin column of grunts I pondered where we might be. This was jungle, but it wasn't the kind of jungle we had encountered around Da Nang. It was a different jungle, a strange jungle. As a corpsman, I wasn't privy to such high-level information as where in the hell we were going or where we were. I just followed along and waited for the inevitable call for service.

We moved like this all day, set in security for the night, then resumed our march the next morning. About noon we came to an unexpected clearing beneath the interlocking branches of the trees. From the sky it would look like jungle, but from the ground it was a base camp. A *huge* base camp. Hundreds of fighting positions dotted the area, camp fires were still burning and tracks in the ground showed where 12.7mm machine guns mounted on wheels had been hastily dragged away. It was obvious that we had almost surprised the NVA in their home. They had deserted the place in such haste that there was not even time to leave booby traps. I was thankful for that. But the question remained: Where did they go? And then the question: Are they coming back?

By the number of prepared positions and camp fires, the force we had surprised vastly outnumbered us. If they attacked the only thing we could do was to try to fight our way out. The skipper quickly came to the conclusion that we could easily find ourselves in a no-win situation—especially if the NVA were now in the process of surrounding our tiny company.

"Listen up," said the captain to the platoon commanders, "we're going to pull back and set up a defensive position. If the gooks decide to attack I want to be ready. If they want us, I want to make sure they take a hell of a beating before they get us."

We cautiously pulled back to a hilltop and began digging in. The captain had picked a good spot to defend. To get to us, the NVA would have to come across an open area, then climb up the steep sides of the hill. Two platoons set up to cover trails at each end of the perimeter. My platoon covered the areas between, reinforced by the gun squad and the CP behind us overlooking our positions.

Night fell turning the jungle so dark that not even shadows could be seen. For hours we stared into the blackness, straining our eyes to catch a hint of movement. The enemy was there. We could sense him but not see him. Sounds of movement in the bush came from one side, then another. It was like they were jockeying for position to attack but couldn't make up their minds to do so. Throughout the night nervous fingers caressed triggers, eyes darted from one black spot to another, attention pulled to one area was quickly diverted to a different one. Why didn't they just attack and get it over with?

Morning came in a bewildering calm. Tensions relaxed with the knowledge that since the NVA had not attacked at night, they would probably not try in the light of day. Then I heard the welcome sound of approaching helicopters. We were being extracted. If any POWs had been there, they were gone now.

We boarded the choppers for the flight back to Da Nang, each man consumed with his own thoughts. It was to be our last major combat operation and we had not even made contact. But we had survived, and that's all that counted. We would be going home soon, and maybe we wouldn't need any more body bags.

In May 1971, combat operations stopped for the Marine Corps in Vietnam. The 1st Marine Division, the last Marine Corps division to leave the Republic of Vietnam, was finally going home. As we boarded helicopters for the last time, for our trip to Hill 34, our "stand-down" hill, I could see fresh army troops being disgorged from other machines to take over our area of responsibility. I felt sorry for them, knowing that before the last American left Vietnam, one of them might become what we feared most—the last man killed.

30

Coming Home

In the spring of 1972, with the majority of American combat units having withdrawn, the North began a full-scale offensive against South Vietnam. The USSR had been reequipping the army of Hanoi with artillery, SAM missiles, tanks, trucks and all the latest military paraphernalia since 1971 in preparation for the invasion. On March 30, it began.

Three widely spaced thrusts cut into South Vietnam in an attempt to disorganize and disintegrate the ARVN, then defeat them in cutoff areas in a piecemeal fashion. The first thrust was across the DMZ into Quang Tri, the second from Cambodia into the Central Highlands to cut the country in half, and the third from southern Cambodia striking straight toward Saigon.

American and South Vietnamese air power managed to blunt, and then finally defeat the offensive. On the ground, the ARVN fought valiantly but without the air support would have stood little chance against the onslaught. With the withdrawal of the 101st Airborne Division on March 10, few American ground combat forces were present during the offensive. On the perimeter at Da Nang was the U.S. 196th

Light Infantry Brigade, backed up by the 84th Engineer Battalion. In Saigon only one brigade remained of the 1st Cavalry Division along with the 1st Aviation Brigade. The 7th Cavalry had left behind one separate brigade, renamed Task Force Garry Owen, at Bien Hoa. These were the last American ground combat units remaining during the Easter Offensive. The era of American servicemen humping the boonies was drawing to a close. For those remaining, waiting for DEROS (Date Eligible for Return from Overseas Service), it was simply a matter of staying alive for a few more months.

In August 1972 that day came. The day when the "Freedom Bird" took the last grunts back to the world. For those who were now going home, the war was over. Or was it?

Many returning veterans would have problems adjusting to civilian life. For many, melding into society would be much tougher than stalking the jungles of Vietnam. At least in Vietnam, they knew the dangers and could usually recognize the enemy—he wore black pajamas or green uniforms and carried weapons. At home the enemy would bear a different face.

Of the 3,402,100 Americans who served in Southeast Asia between 1964 and 1973, almost 2,600,000 served in Vietnam. About 80 percent of those made a successful transition to civilian life, but even many of this number had problems in dealing with the attitudes of an ungrateful nation. Although many were aware of the public's hostility toward the war, few were prepared for the level of resentment leveled against them—simply because they had been there. Little approval or acceptance awaited them and it would be several years before an attitude of understanding would surface within the nation. For the veterans of Vietnam, the war would continue to be a burden much heavier than the rucksacks and weapons they had carried.

For the medics and corpsmen of Vietnam, guilt feelings often ran deep. Instead of thoughts of having killed other human beings, the medics often had emotional problems stemming from a failure in trying to *save* a life. Many exhibited feelings that ranged from blaming the victim—"I tried everything I could and the bastard *still* died on me.

Damn him!"—to a sense of inadequacy: ". . . maybe if someone else was there, someone better than me, someone who could have done more, he might have lived."

These emotions and the lack of understanding and acceptance by society created a unique dilemma for the "Docs." Though they had gone over to save lives, they returned only to find that they, like their grunt counterparts, were tagged "baby killers" and "hooch burners."

Coming home did not mean the war was over.

31

Gary Beikirch
Former Special Forces Medic
October 1973

I looked at the note in bewilderment. It read: Someone from Washington is going to call you tonight at 6 P.M. at the inn.

I wondered what *that* was all about. I had been out of the army for over two years. Surely they didn't want me back. Was I in trouble for something that I didn't know about? I thought about going back into the hills and forgetting about it but my curiosity overwhelmed me. I decided to be at the local inn when the call came.

Civilian life had not agreed with me. I had started college with little money and had to live in a Volkswagen van while on campus. I tried to attend the classes, but people walked up behind me, spit on me, called me "baby killer" and made my life miserable. One day I had had enough. As I walked to class, a young coed—someone I had never even seen before—came up behind me and spit on my back. "Murderer!" she had shouted, anger in her face. She didn't know anything about me except that I had been in Vietnam. That was all that mattered to her. Not my background, not what I had done over there, not even the fact that I went to *save* lives. I just looked at her for a moment, shook my head, walked to my van, started the engine and drove away. I had thought I was ready for college, but college obviously wasn't ready for me.

I made my way into northern New Hampshire and lost myself in the beautiful woodlands of the White Mountains. I hiked, fished and lived off the land. Seeking solitude, I built a camp and settled in. I had a post office box in Lancaster and checked it once a week. Beyond that, I had little contact with the local people. I missed my Montagnards and my friends, but they could not be replaced by people who had not been there—the people of the American lowlands. I began to feel as the Sedang did toward their Vietnamese rivals. *My* lowlanders would never understand.

I had tried to blend in with society on several occasions, but it just didn't work out. I tried to enroll in the newly formed Physician's Assistant program, a course of study designed for former medics and navy corpsmen being conducted at Dartmouth College, but my experiences in Vietnam caught up with me when I met with one of the admission representatives.

"It appears you have the qualifications for the course," said the man, examining my résumé. "Special Forces medic, lots of schools, looks okay. But I've got just one question. How is it you can kill all those people over there, and now want to help people too?"

I lost it. I couldn't believe what I had just heard. I reached across, grabbed him and pulled him over the desk. I wanted to tear him apart, but I knew it wouldn't do any good. I regained my composure, let him go and walked out. So much for PA school.

I applied for a job at a hospital. With all the medical experience I had, surely someone could put it to use. I was *almost* right. They hired me—for the housekeeping department. I was allowed to push brooms, swing mops and run vacuum cleaners. I could wheel oxygen bottles up to the rooms, but wasn't allowed to even hook them up. A nurse had to do that. After all, she was "qualified."

All that was behind me now. At least I thought so until the message about the call from Washington arrived in my mailbox. I went to the inn to await the call. At six o'clock, the phone rang.

"Gary Beikirch?" asked the voice on the phone.

"Yes?"

"Gary, you don't know what we've gone through trying to find you. I'm Major Westmoreland. I'm calling to tell you that you have been awarded the Medal of Honor . . ."

"What?"

"That's right. You *are* the Gary Beikirch who was in the Special Forces at Dak Seang, aren't you?"

"Yes, I was there."

"Then you've got the medal. We want to send an escort up there and bring you down to Washington to meet President Nixon. Can you make it?"

My head spun. I was speechless. Long buried scenes of the battle burst forth and raced through my brain in instant replay. *I* didn't deserve the medal any more than any of the other guys, especially Deo and Tot. *They* had carried me around to treat the wounded and pull them in. Even "Dizzy" Dizzine carried me several times. *Those* guys deserved it. Not me.

"Gary?" asked the major after a few moments of waiting for an answer.

"Uh, I guess so, sir." I decided to take the medal. Not for me, but for Deo, Tot and the other brave warriors of Dak Seang. I would accept it for them. I would wear it for them. *They* earned it.

I stood in line with nine other veterans to receive the Medal of Honor. President Nixon went from man to man, taking each medal, suspended on its blue ribbon, and hanging it around our necks. A smile, a handshake, soon it was over. I felt strange. The medal felt heavy, not by physical weight but by the magnitude of its meaning. Many brave men had gone before us and others would follow, most receiving the medal posthumously. It was a heavy burden to bear and a great responsibility for us.

I took the medal home, put it in my duffel bag with the others I had received an eon before and put it away. It would remain there for two years. Two years of thinking and putting things back together. Finally, after the pain of the attempts to reenter society subsided, I decided to attend the upcoming biannual Medal of Honor convention.

In the hotel room, I took the medal from its case, slowly hung it around my neck and started for the dining room. *This is for Deo and Tot,* I thought as I waited for the elevator, *my friends. I wish you were here.* Then, with an odd feeling, *maybe you are . . .*

And as my mind drifted back to that night at Dak Seang, the sights and sounds again came back to me. Somewhere in the distance, perhaps from the long-buried recesses of my memory, I could hear one word echo faintly at first, then again a bit louder:

Medic!

32

Afterward

In the years following their return from Vietnam, the "Docs" who shared their experiences with the author overcame numerous obstacles in taking their place in society, and each, in his own way, came through not only their trial by fire, but the trials of life.

At the time of this writing only three of the medics and corpsmen whose stories appear on these pages remain in the medical field. For those who entered other occupations, like their brothers who stayed with medicine, a desire to help people continued to influence their selection of careers.

James Callahan works for the Massachusetts Turnpike Authority and is active in the Pittsfield Chapter of the Vietnam Veterans of America.

Mike Stout is physically disabled and lives in a comfortable country home in Glencoe, Oklahoma. Callahan and Stout were reunited twenty-one years after the battle in the clearing during Operation Billings as a result of the research for this book.

Dennis Chaney now lives in Monrovia, California, and works in an administrative position in a local hospital.

Douglas Wean is a section supervisor in the X-ray section at the Hines VA hospital in Hines (Chicago), Illinois. He also teaches clinical X-ray techniques at the College of DuPage and is active in the 3rd Marine Division Association.

Bill Wells is a career police officer and has attained the rank of lieutenant with the Tulsa, Oklahoma, police department.

Bob Bosma lives on the campus of Kemper Military Academy in Boonville, Missouri, where he serves as a tactical officer for the Junior High Cadet Company. He is currently forming a national association for Vietnam medics and corpsmen and is still active in the military, holding the rank of sergeant first class in the Army Reserve. His assignment is medical operations sergeant at the Fort Rucker Army Hospital.

Stephen Bass is a career police officer with the Tulsa Police Department and maintains a second career in the Army Reserve as a captain in the Medical Service Corps.

Tim Roth stayed in the medical field and is a physician's assistant at VA Medical Center in San Francisco, California.

Leonard Finnell is a detective with the Tulsa Police Department working in the forgery squad.

Gary Beikirch went to seminary school, received his Master's degree, served as a pastor of a church and a counselor at a veterans' outreach center. His desire to work with children culminated in his present position as a school counselor for a middle school in Rochester, New York, working with sixth-, seventh- and eighth-graders.

Of the U.S. Navy medical corpsmen who served with the Marines in Vietnam, 3 won the Medal of Honor for their actions. The Navy Cross was awarded to 29, the Silver Star to 107, and 4,563 received the Purple Heart for wounds received in action. Separate statistics were not kept by the navy for the number of corpsmen killed in action.

U.S. Army medics accounted for 14 Medals of Honor. But the cost was high. Over thirteen hundred Army medics in Vietnam lost their lives during the war.

> . . . 'E carried me away
> To where a dooli* lay,
> An' a bullet come an' drilled the beggar clean.
> 'E put me safe inside,
> An' just before 'e died,
> "I 'ope you liked your drink," sez Gunga Din . . .

—Rudyard Kipling, *Gunga Din*

---

*Ambulance cart

Citations

Gary B. Beikirch

Company B, 5th Special Forces Group, 1st Special Forces, Kontum Province, Republic of Vietnam, 1 April 1970.

Award: Medal of Honor
Citation:

For conspicuous gallantry and intrepidity in action at the risk of his life above and beyond the call of duty. Sergeant Beikirch, medical aidman, Detachment B-24, Company B, distinguished himself during the defense of Camp Dak Seang. The allied defenders suffered a number of casualties as a result of an intense, devastating attack launched by the enemy from well-concealed positions surrounding the camp. Sergeant Beikirch, with complete disregard for his personal safety, moved unhesitatingly through the withering enemy fire to his fallen comrades, applied first aid to their wounds and assisted them to the medical aid station. When

CITATIONS

informed that a seriously injured American officer was lying in an exposed position, Sergeant Beikirch ran immediately through the hail of fire. Although he was wounded seriously by fragments from an exploding enemy shell, Sergeant Beikirch carried the officer to a medical aid station. Ignoring his own serious injuries, Sergeant Beikirch left the relative safety of the medical bunker to search for and evacuate other men who had been injured. He was again wounded as he dragged a critically injured Vietnamese soldier to the medical bunker while simultaneously applying mouth-to-mouth resuscitation to sustain his life. Sergeant Beikirch again refused treatment and continued his search for other casualties until he collapsed. Only then did he permit himself to be treated. Sergeant Beikirch's complete devotion to the welfare of his comrades, at the risk of his life is in keeping with the highest traditions of the military service and reflects great credit on him, his unit and the U.S. Army.

Douglas Louis Wean

Battery K, 4th Battalion, 12th Marines, 9th Marine Amphibious Brigade, Quang Tri Province, Republic of Vietnam, 19 September 1968.

Award: Silver Star Medal
Citation:

For conspicuous gallantry and intrepidity in action while serving as a corpsman with Battery K, 4th Battalion, 12th Marines, 9th Marine Amphibious Brigade in connection with operations against the enemy in the Republic of Vietnam. On the morning of 19 September 1968, while occupying a fire support position at the Rockpile in Quang Tri Province, Petty Officer Wean's platoon came under a heavy volume of North Vietnamese artillery fire. During the ensuing attack, several rounds impacted in the powder storage area, wounding numerous Marines and igniting an intense fire which rapidly spread to other storage points. Responding instantly to a call for medical assistance, Petty Officer Wean unhesitatingly left his position of relative safety and rushed across the fire-swept terrain to the side of a wounded comrade. Ignoring the fragmentation of exploding ordnance and the enemy rounds impacting near him, he shielded the injured Marine with his own body while calmly administering medical aid to the casualty. When the wounded man was evacuated to the battalion aid station, Petty Officer Wean fearlessly moved to another wounded comrade and skillfully treated the man's wounds, until he was extracted from the hazardous area. His heroic actions and sincere concern for the welfare of his comrades inspired all who observed him and were instrumental in saving the lives of two Marines. By his courage, resolute determination and steadfast devotion to duty in the face of great personal danger, Petty Officer Wean upheld the highest traditions of the Marine Corps and of the United States Naval Service.

Michael O. Stout

Alpha Company, 2nd Battalion, 28th Infantry, 1st Infantry Division.

Award: Silver Star Medal
Citation:

For gallantry in action against a hostile force (on 17 June 1967). On this date, during Operation Billings, Specialist Stout was serving as a medical aidman for his unit which was conducting a search and destroy mission deep in a Vietcong infested area of War Zone D. While establishing a night defensive position, they were suddenly subjected to intense small arms and automatic weapons fire from an estimated Vietcong battalion. During the first few moments of action, Specialist Stout's unit sustained numerous casualties. Despite the heavy enemy fire, Specialist Stout unhesitatingly moved forward to administer aid to the wounded. When he discovered several wounded men lying immobile in an open area, Specialist Stout, with complete disregard for his personal safety, ran to them, quickly administered first aid and dragged each of the men to safety. He then organized litter teams to carry the wounded to the evacuation site. Specialist Stout continued to move about the area with complete disregard for the enemy fire as he searched for and treated other casualties until the Vietcong had been routed and all the wounded had been cared for. Specialist Stout's outstanding courage and resolution of purpose were directly responsible for saving the lives of many of his comrades. Specialist Four Stout's unquestionable valor while engaged in military operations involving conflict with an insurgent force is in keeping with the finest traditions of the military service and reflects great credit upon himself, the 1st Infantry Division and the United States Army.

Stephen J. Bass

Headquarters Company, 69th Engineer Battalion, 20th Engineer Brigade, Can Tho Army Airfield, Phong Dinh Province, Republic of Vietnam, 13 January 1969.

Award: Bronze Star Medal for Heroism
Citation:

At 0230 hours the Can Tho Army Airfield came under rocket attack and ground attack by a Vietcong sapper force of indeterminate size. The attackers successfully penetrated the base perimeter and overran a command bunker. During the ensuing firefight, casualties mounted rapidly and medics were called out to aid the wounded. Specialist Bass repeatedly went to the areas under attack despite the fact that these areas were not secure to friendly forces. Without radio contact to inform his ambulance team of the current tactical situation, he continued to return to the thick of the battle, evacuating the seriously wounded and administering first aid. In one instance he responded to cries from a command bunker, unaware that it had fallen under enemy control, and was driven back by intense fire from the bunker. Undaunted, Specialist Five Bass continued to lead his ambulance team under fire in scouring the perimeter for wounded personnel. Upon the restoration of security to the perimeter, Specialist Bass returned to the airfield dispensary and rendered invaluable assistance to the doctors and prepared the more seriously wounded for helicopter evacuation. His total disregard for his own personal safety and exemplary dedication to the preservation of human life were in keeping with the highest traditions of the military service and reflect great credit upon himself, his unit and the United States Army.

Robert E. Bosma

Battery C, 1st Battalion, 77th Artillery, 1st Cavalry Division (Airmobile), Hue City, Thua Thien Province, Republic of Vietnam, 3 January 1968.

Award: Army Commendation Medal for Heroism
Citation:

For heroism in connection with military operations against a hostile force in the Republic of Vietnam. Private First Class Bosma distinguished himself by heroism in action on 3 January 1968, while serving as a medical aidman with Battery C, 1st Battalion, 77th Artillery during a combat mission in the Republic of Vietnam. When his unit became heavily engaged with a large enemy force, Private First Class Bosma exposed himself to the hostile fire as he administered first aid and evacuated his wounded comrades to safety. His display of personal bravery and devotion to duty is in keeping with the highest traditions of the military service, and reflects great credit upon himself, his unit and the United States Army.

Appendix

A Short History of the Field Medical Soldier

Over the course of the war in Vietnam, 303,704 Americans were wounded as a result of enemy action. Of this number, those losing at least one limb totaled more than all those in World War II and Korea combined. Almost one-third of those wounded in battle came home with a permanent physical disability.

It could have been worse. Because of the efficient and timely treatment afforded by the field medics and corpsmen, the speedy evacuation—usually by helicopter—and the advanced medical services provided in the rear area hospitals, 82 percent of those wounded in action survived. In comparison to wars of the past, this number was remarkable.

Throughout history, armies and navies have attempted to provide some means of caring for their wounded. In the wars of ancient Greece and Rome, those who fell in battle were removed and cared for by camp followers—usually women who doubled as cooks, food foragers and companions of the soldier—or family members who traveled with the army. The few physicians available knew little of internal medicine and care of traumatic injuries fell into two categories: those that could heal naturally with the aid of bandages, and the more serious that would have to be cauterized. Beyond this, it was left up to the wounded to recover on their own. Infection became as great a killer as the enemy.

During the Crusades, a military order of monks was formed by the Church to care for the wounded. This was the first time that a specialized organization was formed whose sole purpose was to provide medical care to an army in the field.

The Siege of Málaga in 1487 saw the first use of the field ambulance. Carts known as *ambulancias* were designated to remove casualties from the field and transport them to a safe rear area for what treatment the physicians of the day could provide. But the surgeons were few and most were designated to care for only the senior officers. During the reign of Edward II, there was only one "chirurgeon" (surgeon) for every 1,900 soldiers.

When Edward III besieged Calais, his entire army had only one physician. Henry V's military code listed surgeons just above washerwomen—and below tailors and shoemakers. Even as late as the reign of Queen Elizabeth I, surgeons held no higher status than that of the drummers. It was not until the advent of gunpowder that medical care began to improve. But medicine was still in its infancy and surgical procedures were rudimentary. For gunshots, treatment consisted of cauterization followed by balms made from various mixtures of oils and herbs. One account even describes a concoction of "two young whelps boiled alive and two pounds of earthworms purified in white wine." Bleeding after amputation was stopped with a poultice of boiling pitch.

The first regimental hospital system came about with the formation of a standing British army. Staffed by regimental surgeons, the medical personnel accompanied the expeditionary forces to the far reaches of the empire. But still, little support was given to the medical system by the senior officers of the army. When the Duke of Wellington, during his advance to Salamanca, was advised to set aside vehicles for transportation of casualties to the hospitals, he refused. In his opinion, vehicles should be used to transport troops and supplies to the battle. The wounded could wait until the battle was over to be sorted out. His inspector of hospitals, Sir James McGrigor, disagreed and managed to provide transport for the wounded on commissary vehicles returning for more supplies. The hospitals he set up along the route of march were assembled from preconstructed sections built in England and sent to the Continent. These became the first prefabricated military field hospitals to follow an army to war.

The American Revolutionary War saw the beginning of the American Army Medical Service. Following the Battle of Bunker Hill, wounded Colonial troops littered the streets of Boston and no provisions had been made to care for them. For three days the wounded cried out in pain, many dying where they lay, until the people of Boston demanded of the British military governor of Massachusetts, General Gage, that something be done. With public sentiment rapidly turning into a powder keg, Gage established hospitals in several private homes.

In July 1775, one month after the battle, the Continental Congress appointed Gen. George Washington commander in chief of the Continental Army. With this appointment came the responsibility of establishing a general staff, but no provision for a medical department. But after Washington took command he quickly saw the need of a medical and hospital program to provide care for the wounded. On July 21, he wrote a letter to the president of the Congress, and in it mentioned: "I have made enquiry into the establishment of the hospital and find it in a very unsettled condition. I could wish it was immediately taken into consideration as the lives and health of both officers and men so much depend on a due regulation of this department."

Though there was little money to support the project, Congress authorized "an hospital" for the twenty thousand-man army with a staff that consisted of a director general, a

217

chief physician, four surgeons, twenty surgeon's mates, one apothecary, a clerk, two storekeepers and a nurse for every ten patients. But there still was no provision to designate personnel to treat the wounded on the battlefield.

It soon became apparent that one hospital was not enough. Each regiment began setting up its own hospitals, usually a two-room log cabin, which could hold between ten and twenty casualties. To assist in the hospital, "medical soldiers" were designated as they were needed—often for one day at a time. Most soldiers did not want to serve in this position and considered it much akin to an undesirable detail verging on punishment. Only the most severely wounded or sick were sent to the hospital, and none were segregated. Soldiers who arrived for treatment of wounds often caught fatal diseases from being contaminated by those who were sent for illnesses. Typhoid, pneumonia, tuberculosis and cholera were rampant, and there was no knowledge of hygiene or diagnosis. Outside the hospitals, many wounded were simply evacuated to local farmers' homes where they were tended by the farmer's family.

After America gained independence, the army medical services faded into oblivion. It was not until the War of 1812 that hospitals and medical care again appeared in military service. But little progress had been made in medical technology and the troops suffered greatly. Dr. William Beaumont, an army doctor who pioneered studies in gastroenterology, wrote of one experience in a makeshift hospital following a battle with the British: "A most distressing scene ensues in the hospital—nothing but the groans of the wounded and agonies of the dying are to be heard. The surgeons wading in blood, cutting off arms, legs and trepanning heads to rescue their fellow creatures from untimely death. To hear the poor creatures crying, 'Oh, dear! . . . Oh, my God! . . . Do, Doctor, Doctor! Do cut off my leg, my arm, my head to relieve me from misery! I can't stand it! I can't live!' would have rent the heart of steel, and shocked the insensibility of the most hardened assassin and the cruelest savage. It awoke my liveliest sympathy and I cut and slashed for forty-eight hours without food or sleep."

After these experiences, Dr. Beaumont devised and proposed a portable tent-type field hospital to accompany the armies in the field. And for the first time, army medical personnel were designated and given distinctive uniforms. But it wasn't until 1851 that hospital stewards, enlisted forerunners of modern army medics, were authorized a branch emblem—a green *caduceus* embroidered to the sleeve of their tunics.

Military medicine in Europe showed little progress over that in America. When England and France went to war against Russia in the Crimea in 1854, medical care was almost nonexistent. When word returned to England of the suffering and deaths due to lack of medical care and supplies, the people were infuriated. After a great hue and cry, Queen Victoria's secretary of war asked a thirty-three-year-old London nurse to form a corps of nurses for duty in the Crimea. In the fall of that same year, Florence Nightingale sailed with thirty-eight nurses for the Mediterranean.

Arriving at Scutari, across from Constantinople (now Istanbul), the nurses in gray uniforms were shocked at what awaited them. In an old Turkish hospital, five hundred wounded survivors of the Battle of Balaclava—including those from the Charge of the Light Brigade—lay in squalor. The blood-soaked bandages had not been changed for days, dirt and trash littered the floor and medical supplies were almost nonexistent. There were no cots, mattresses or bandages, and few men were well enough to assist the nurses with the cleanup and care of the more seriously wounded. Still, within days, the small band of nurses, by working day and night, turned the dilapidated barracks into a useable army hospital.

But too many men died before they could reach the hospital. It was obvious to Nurse Nightingale that more lives could be saved if medical care could be provided *on* the battlefield. She traveled to the front to investigate the possibility of forming a medical service in the field, but contracted Crimean fever shortly after arrival and nearly died. She returned to Scutari and recovered, but the war ended before the prospect of an organized medical service in the field could materialize.

Five years later America found herself again at war—a

war where every casualty was an American. At no time in history had America encountered the number of casualties the Civil War produced. Men wounded in battle were simply removed to hospital tents or nearby buildings where doctors, for lack of medications to counter gangrene, performed amputations on limbs that often only had minor wounds—and without any anesthetic beyond an occasional bottle of whiskey. Sterilizing surgical instruments was still unheard of, and overworked doctors seldom even bothered to wash their hands before moving on to the next casualty. Infection was rampant, but even more appalling were the deaths during the war due to disease. It is estimated that for every death due to battle wounds, 2.5 men died of disease.

As the number of casualties mounted on both sides, military medicine expanded more rapidly than in any previous period of history. Confederate surgeon James Brown McCaw headed the Chimborazo Hospital near Richmond that contained nine thousand beds and became the largest military hospital on either side during the war. Yet, because of lack of attention on the battlefield, when it is most critical, 50,000 of the 600,000 Confederate soldiers mobilized for the war died of wounds and a further 150,000 of diseases. The Union Army fared worse with 110,070 dying from wounds and 224,586 from disease.

In 1861 a nurse named Clara Barton began delivering medical supplies to Union troops and nursing the wounded in the field. Known as "The Angel of the Battlefield," Barton drew the attention of the U.S. government which, in 1864, appointed her superintendent of nurses for the Army of the James. Yet, other than male hospital attendants—usually soldiers unfit for duty in the field—no enlisted male medical specialists existed. With the numbers of wounded increasing at an alarming rate and few being returned to the regiments for duty, it quickly became obvious that something would have to be done to curtail the continual depletion of men from the ranks. The solution called for the permanent formation of an enlisted hospital corps of members specifically trained for hospital duty. In 1862 Gen. William H. Hammond announced that formation of such an organization would release several thousand soldiers serving in a detached status to the hospitals to be returned to their regiments. The recommendation was approved and the first permanent hospital corps came into being with each enlisted member holding the rank of sergeant. But still, after almost two years of fighting, no provisions had been made for evacuation of wounded from the battlefield.

Finally, Assistant Surgeon Jonathan Letterman, medical director of the Union Army of the Potomac, established the first system of removing the wounded from the field. He had seen soldiers wounded during the Battle of Bull Run lie at the front for up to a week and finally die for lack of medical care. To him, this was unacceptable. He devised a tiered system that included field aid stations, ambulances, field hospitals, hospital trains and general hospitals. His ideas were first tested at the Battle of Antietam, and worked so well that the system was officially adopted by the Union Army in 1864 and remained the standard through the Spanish-American War. Evacuation of the wounded began when the litter bearers picked up the casualty from where he fell and carried him to the aid station. Field ambulances transported the more serious cases to collection points for medical clearing. From there, they were transported to field hospitals or general hospitals depending on the severity of their wounds. This method of triage became the basis of the modern evacuation system.

In 1869 Clara Barton, after her experiences in the Civil War, traveled to Europe to help nurse those wounded during the Franco-Prussian War and there witnessed the work done by the International Committee of the Red Cross. Seeing the effectiveness of an organized civilian field medical service in assisting with battle casualties, Barton returned to the U.S. in 1879 and immediately began campaigning for establishment of an American branch of the Red Cross. Two years later the American Red Cross came into being and for the first time the army would have an organized system of medical support from the civilian sector.

During the 1870s and 1880s army medical soldiers accompanied the cavalry regiments as America forged westward. It has been recorded that one army medic rode with

Custer into the Little Big Horn. And as the army posts were established to protect settlers during the westward expansion, medical personnel were assigned to the forts to work in the dispensary. For the doctors and hospital attendants—often only private soldiers detailed for extra duty from the companies—the work was routinely accomplished under the most primitive of conditions.

Private H. Habers, a hospital steward serving with a cavalry troop on the frontier, left a diary that described what his job was like. In it he describes an incident that took place while his troop was on its way to its new post, Fort Dodge, Kansas. During the march to the fort the troop came to the banks of the rain-swollen Arkansas River. No bridge existed, so one brave soul had to swim through the muddy water to the other side with a rope tied to his waist. The rope was made taut and each soldier crossed hand-over-hand, pulling on the reins of their swimming horses, until all reached the opposite bank where they made camp for the night.

The next morning, since the river water was too salty to drink, the troop moved out toward a water hole where "sweet" water could be found—a distance of some fifteen miles. Along the way they hunted game with their single-shot Springfield breech-loaders and, under the guidance of the hospital steward, foraged for wild vegetables such as garlic and lamb's-quarter (similar to collard greens) to counter scurvy. When they finally reached the fort, Habers made his way wearily to his barracks within the stockade—a room described as simply having a dirt floor and wooden bunk beds with straw mattresses.

Still, the fort did offer protection against the frequent Indian attacks. On one such occasion, a band of marauding Indians "aroused the garrison" by setting fire to the prairie grass outside the fort—something they did quite often. No well existed within the fort and the only water about had to be hauled into the fort from a nearby creek. The soldiers, in order to protect the dry tinderbox structure, were forced to beat the fire out with burlap feed bags. As they exposed themselves to accomplish this task they came under fire from the Indians who had used the fire not only in an attempt to destroy the fort, but to draw out the soldiers into an ambush zone.

All within and without the garrison became pinned down as they returned fire. Habers, since there were not enough weapons to go around, found himself lying on the floor of one room amidst an ever-growing pile of empty cartridge cases as the soldiers at the window fought desperately to repulse the attack. Finally the firing slackened and the Indians withdrew.

Habers darted out onto the battleground to check for casualties. Within minutes he found a sergeant, two arrows stuck in his neck, hiding underneath a haystack.

Private Habers carried the sergeant back to the dispensary where, with no mention of anesthetic, he began to work. His diary only makes simple note: "I extracted the arrows. The patient recovered nicely." One can only imagine what it must have been like that day in the crude "operating room."

By this time anesthetic was not unknown in the medical field. As early as 1800 nitrous oxide, or "laughing gas," had been recognized as having anesthetic qualities. But these properties were not experimented with until 1844 when Dr. Horace Wells, an American dentist, used it on himself while having a tooth pulled.

In 1842 another anesthetic, vapor of ether, was used by an American doctor named Crawford W. Long to successfully render a patient unconscious. But Long did not publish his findings and credit for the discovery of anesthesia went to a Boston dentist, Dr. W.T.G. Morton, in 1846.

Sir James Y. Simpson, a Scottish physician, used chloroform to ease the pain of childbirth as early as 1847. The technique was so successful that Queen Victoria herself was anesthetized in this fashion during delivery.

But one form of anesthesia that surfaced during the Civil War would accompany fighting men wounded in the field well into the twentieth century. Imported from China, Turkey and Greece was a derivative of the opium poppy refined into a chemical known as morphia. This chemical, because of its amazing capability to quickly reduce pain and quiet a patient, was medically dubbed "heroin" for its "heroic" qualities. Though it wasn't carried into the field, it was used in some hospitals prior to surgery. It was not until after the war that the addictive power of this drug was determined detrimental. Yet, opium derivatives continued to serve as pain relievers for trauma victims, the most common coming into use in World War I in the form of morphine—a drug that would see service to the present day.

Besides anesthesia, other advancements were being made in the civilian medical fields between 1860 and 1880. But in the military, innovations in medicine were slow to arrive and recognition of the need for a designated medical corps took back seat to the political and budgetary requirements of the Cavalry, Artillery and Infantry. It wasn't until 1887 that the need for an Army Medical Department was finally recognized and formally organized as a separate entity. Then four years later, to address the need to provide enlisted medical soldiers to the Army hospitals and field units, the first school for the Hospital Corps was organized by Colonel John Van Rensselaer Hoff at Fort Riley, Kansas. The Army medic, though few in numbers, had finally been given a permanent branch.

In 1898 war with Spain erupted with the sinking of the U.S. battleship *Maine*. The fledgling Army Medical Department found itself sadly unprepared for a war on foreign soil. Each regiment had only one surgeon, two assistants and less than ten hospital stewards. And as in past wars, disease claimed more victims than bullets. Yellow fever, known as "Yellow Jack" by the soldiers in Cuba, and typhoid fever counted for over 3,500 deaths. The conquering of the dreaded yellow fever is attributed to the legendary army major Walter Reed. But few people know that it was an army medic, Private John Kissinger, who volunteered to serve as the test case to prove that the disease was transmitted by mosquitos. He courageously allowed himself to be bitten by infected mosquitos on three separate occasions until he contracted the disease. Now with proof positive, a mosquito eradication program was established that curtailed the epidemic. Walter Reed later said of Kissinger: "In my opinion, this exhibition of moral courage has never been surpassed in the annals of the Army of the United States." Kissinger recovered and was discharged from the army in

1901 with the notation on his discharge: "Character—excellent."

Realizing in 1914, with the outbreak of war in Europe, that America stood a good chance of entering the conflict, the Army Medical Department began to prepare. By 1918, when America entered the war, the service consisted of 833 physicians, 86 dentists, 403 nurses, 62 veterinarians and *6,619* enlisted medics. Also established prior to deployment overseas was a Sanitary Corps, consisting of enlisted personnel trained to eliminate disease hazards. World War I became the first war in which deaths due to disease were less than those of battle.

The Army Medical Corps with its field medics, litter bearers and ambulance drivers, was the first American military unit to arrive in Europe. As unarmed noncombatants, the field medics of the army suffered greatly due to their determination to stay close to the fighting men. By war's end, 2,257 medics had been killed in action or died from wounds or disease. Of these, Pfc. Oscar C. Tugo, an enlisted field medic, was the first American killed in action in the war.

World War I proved the necessity of having enlisted medics in the field. By the time the troops returned home, it was well established that the best time to begin saving a man's life was when he fell—*on the battleground!* For this to be possible medics would have to be attached to the combat units down to company level. Instead of aid stations in the trenches and litter bearers to retrieve the wounded, the medics would accompany the fighting men when they went into action.

When America entered World War II, this practice was well in place and medics served in every combat unit in the war. Though in 1939 the Army Medical Department could only count a total of 2,181 assigned personnel, by D day in June of 1944 army enlisted medics alone numbered 553,095. These unarmed noncombatants who wore the distinctive red cross emblazoned on a white background on their helmets and sleeve brassards acquitted themselves heroically. By war's end, eight army medics had won Medals of Honor. But their dedication was costly. Among the

Americans killed in action in Europe, 3,061 were enlisted army medics.

Five years after the end of World War II army medics once again found themselves on the field of battle. North Korea invaded the south in 1950 and America, as part of the United Nations force sent to repel the invaders, would spend three years fighting through the rugged mountains, oppressive heat and freezing cold of that Asian land. Wherever the fighting man went, Doc was with him.

A soldier wounded in Korea stood an even better chance of survival than his WWII counterparts. With the advent of the helicopter ambulance, a casualty could be evacuated from places wheeled ambulances could not reach and be transported to a MASH (Mobile Army Surgical Hospital) within a matter of minutes instead of hours. This asset would prove invaluable in Vietnam.

The history of the navy medical corpsman paralleled that of the army. As early as Roman times, certain seamen, called *Immunes,* cared for the sick and wounded. The writings of Homer make reference to physicians sailing with the Greek fleets whose main duty was sanitation officer. The Greeks felt that disease was somehow linked to lack of cleanliness—an idea that was forgotten by the Middle Ages when the Black Death (bubonic plague) manifested itself in Europe after arriving aboard ships returning from Asia Minor.

As with the land-based armies, the navies of the world encountered more deaths due to disease than to battle. Scurvy—later found to be the most easily treated of all diseases—accounted for the majority of deaths at sea. One sixteenth-century naval captain, Sir John Hawkins, reported that in his twenty years of service, scurvy alone killed over twenty thousand sailors of the British navy. During Magellan's circumnavigation of the world in 1522 all but eighteen crewmen died of the dreaded disease. It wasn't until 1747 that a British naval surgeon, Dr. James Lind, proved that certain fruits—especially limes—curtailed the disease. But fifty years would pass before the drinking of lime juice would be required aboard all British vessels.

The first definite record of naval enlisted personnel serving in the medical field was written in 1512. Aboard the ships of Henry VIII, a commissioned ship's doctor and enlisted surgeon's mates manned the sick berth or "sick bay." Dubbed "loblollys" because of the porridge they fed the sick, these surgeon's mates were normally ship's cooks and cabin boys who worked with the surgeon as a second duty assignment. These duties and assignments remained standard throughout the navies of the world until the Revolutionary War.

On June 1, 1778, a seaman named John Wall was recruited to serve aboard the American frigate *Constellation* as a full-time surgeon's mate, becoming the first enlisted person to serve as a permanent medical aide in the U.S. Navy. In March of 1779, an act of Congress was passed establishing the Medical Department of the Navy. By this time, enlisted medical personnel served in every ship of the line.

In 1842, the term *loblolly boy* was replaced with the designation of surgeon's steward. Along with the new title, the selection process changed. Ships' doctors selected their men for their ". . . knowledge of pharmacy and ordinary accounts," and they had to be "of industrious and temperate habits."

In the Civil War, male nurses and surgeon's stewards served on both Union and Confederate ships. But unlike their army counterparts, they seldom went ashore to support landing forces. In 1866 the rating of surgeon's steward was replaced by "apothecary" and the caduceus became the designated emblem to be worn on the uniform sleeve.

The Hospital Corps was organized as a separate unit by act of Congress on June 17, 1898. Two years later, a navy corpsman, Hospital Apprentice Robert Standley, accompanied the relief expedition overland to Peking during the Boxer Rebellion. During this action, Standley became the first navy corpsman to win the Medal of Honor.

Navy corpsmen served in the field with the Marines in World War I during the battles of Château-Thierry, Soissons, Saint-Mihiel and Belleau Wood. For these actions, the field corpsmen became the most highly decorated U.S. Navy unit of the war. In one action in September 1918, the army's 89th Division assaulted the town of Xammes to unseat the German defenders thought to be well entrenched and ready for battle. They were shocked to find the town already occupied by navy corpsmen who had arrived the day before to set up an aid station "closer to the action."

During the same advance, a navy corpsman with the 6th Marine Regiment witnessed a Marine struck by enemy fire fall in an open field. Without hesitation, Hospital Apprentice First Class David E. Hayden raced across the fire-swept ground to treat the wounded Marine. Bullets raked the ground and laced the air as he applied bandages, but he never faltered. As the Marines watched, Hayden picked up the casualty and carried him through a hail of bullets to safety. The observers were incredulous that Hayden wasn't killed. For his actions, Hayden received the Medal of Honor.

By the end of the war, the Hospital Corps had received numerous citations from both the United States and France. Those serving with the Marines were the only naval personnel permitted to wear the French Fourrege, an award given to only the most valorous units.

Corpsmen attached to the Marines in the Pacific during World War II served in every island battle the Marines fought. Numerous accounts of their courage under fire have been written but none could adequately describe the way the Marines felt about their "Docs." Gen. Lewis C. Walt, who was a young lieutenant during the Guadalcanal campaign came closest when he wrote: "I can't say enough to praise them . . . They out-Marine a Marine by volunteering for all kinds of jobs, including more than their share of patrols . . . They are proud and dedicated and the Marines think the world of them. Why, a Marine platoon would no more go into battle without corpsmen than without weapons. The fact that they know corpsmen are there to take care of them is a tremendous morale factor."

Guadalcanal, Tulagi, Tarawa, Saipan, Iwo Jima, Okinawa . . . names that burned into the annals of Marine Corps history, names that cost American lives and blood, would have been far more costly had it not been for the intrepid corpsmen who stood side by side with the fighting men. And the Marines will never forget. For the most famous photograph in Marine Corps history—the flag raising on Mount Suribachi during the battle for Iwo Jima—shows six men grasping the pole as it is being planted. Five are Marines, but one—John H. Bradley—was a navy corpsman.

By the end of the war, corpsmen assigned to the Marines had accumulated 464 Silver Star Medals, 25 Navy Crosses and 7 Medals of Honor. But the cost was horrendous. Of the corpsmen who served in the field, 1,724 died of wounds and disease and 889 were killed in action.

For the corpsmen in Korea, activities in the field were closely akin to their army counterparts. Gunshot and shrapnel wounds, dysentery, and in the winter, overwhelming cases of frostbite, were daily occurrences. And like the army, medical evacuation techniques entered a new age. No longer would a casualty face hours, and sometimes even days, before hospital treatment could be effected. Military field medicine had finally reached a standard that was both efficient and expedient.

Never again would the lonely soldier, wounded and left to his own means, be forced to follow Rudyard Kipling's advice to *The Young British Soldier:*

When you're wounded and left on Afghanistan's plains,
And the women come out to cut up what remains,
Just roll to your rifle and blow out your brains,
An' go to your Gawd like a soldier . . .

Bibliography

Adams, George W. *Doctors in Blue; The Medical History of the Union Army in the Civil War.* New York: Henry Schuman, 1952.

Ashburn, P.M. *A History of the Medical Department of the United States Army.* New York: Houghton Mifflin Co., 1929.

Engle, Eloise Katherine. *Medic.* New York: John Day Co., 1967.

Gillett, Mary C. *The Army Medical Department, 1818–1865.* Center of Military History, United States Army, 1987.

History of the Hospital Corps. Handbook of the Hospital Corps, United States Navy, 1962.

BIBLIOGRAPHY

Hume, Edgar Erskine. *Victories of Army Medicine.* Philadelphia, PA: J. B. Lippincott Co., 1943.

Tobey, James A. *The Medical Department of the Army; Its History, Activities and Organization.* Baltimore: Johns Hopkins Press, 1927.